Shhh, Hypnotic Work in Progress

Shhh, Hypnotic Work in Progress

Twelve Case Histories in Clinical Hypnotherapy

Randy J. Hartman, M.A.

Writers Club Press
San Jose New York Lincoln Shanghai

Shhh, Hypnotic Work in Progress
Twelve Case Histories in Clinical Hypnotherapy

Writers Club Press
an imprint of iUniverse.com, Inc.

For information address:
iUniverse.com, Inc.
620 North 48th Street, Suite 201
Lincoln, NE 68504-3467
www.iuniverse.com

ISBN: 0-595-14188-9

Printed in the United States of America

Contents

◆

Forward

◆

Shhh, Hypnotic Work in Progress…Twelve Case Histories in Clinical Hypnotherapy was very exciting and informative to read. This book depicts the expertise of Randy Hartman in each of the twelve case histories related in this book. Randy's understanding of how Dr Milton Erickson methodically and precisely engineered and designed methods to deal with individuals suffering from past and present problems is like having your own personal mentor in book form. The brain is a very powerful organ in one's body that can be used as a natural healing tool for physical, emotional, and psychological pain. Through the use of hypnotherapy, Randy has clearly and successfully used this mode of therapy to contact the subconscious mind of each subject and has delineated in a clear and step-by-step manner how he dealt with each one.

Randy Hartman is clearly an ambassador in this field of clinical hypnotherapy. His desire to learn and utilize the caring and non-threatening methods of Dr. Milton Erickson has been clearly accomplished. Through this book of twelve case histories and his previous book on metaphors titled Trance Scripts, Randy has unselfishly given to his readers methods to deal with their patients and even themselves in a very powerful and successful manner. I would like to personally thank Randy at this time for all he has taught me in the field of clinical hypnotherapy. Hypnotherapy is a very exciting and successful therapeutic tool to utilize.

Ronald C. Gorman, M.A, CDSIII, C.H.

Introduction

◆

The intent of this book is to provide a framework for other clinical hypnotherapists to use and later develop their own unique approaches. Hypnotherapy has to be tailored to meet the needs of the individual patient if it is to be truly effective. With that thought I strongly encourage my colleagues, experienced and inexperienced alike to use references like this book as a framework or a springboard if you will, toward designing more effective treatment interventions on a case by case basis.

I cannot say that my way of doing a clinical hypnotic intervention is the right approach for all patients, but these interventions have worked well with the individual patients in this book. From my field of experience I have found that the most powerful hypnotic interventions were the ones designed just for that specific patient to meet their desired outcome. It is all to easy for the hypnotherapists own agenda to prescribe and try to control the outcome for the patient. The only successful outcome is the one that the patient desires, not the desire of the hypnotherapist. Over the years I have come to the conclusion that there is not any area of human functioning that hypnosis cannot have a tremendous impact on, providing the patient does desire change.

If you truly want to understand something in your life, or the life of others, just attempt to change it. Clinical hypnosis will not only help you with trying to make those changes, but it will also facilitate a greater learning experience for you. Any person that tells me they know all there is to know about human behavior and hypnosis would surely have to be a fool. Clinical hypnosis is not only a great therapeutic tool, but also a true adventure in the field of therapy. It is a language therapy that can penetrate the subconscious mind and can assist in altering many of the human body functions and emotional responses. It is this sleeping giant known as clinical hypnosis that can put incredible power in your hands, power over habits, fears, tensions, stress, pain, confidence, even your physical state of well being. Clinical hypnosis has helped me, and if you will allow it, clinical hypnosis can help you.

The one person I have the most trouble working with for change is "me". Probably the most difficult patient you will ever encounter will no doubt be yourself! It is wise to remember that an error in behavior does not become a mistake until you refuse to correct it. At every possible opportunity I want to continue to urge all hypnotherapists to exercise their utmost flexibility to meet their patients needs.

Dedication

◆

This book was first written in June 1992 in Olympia, Washington. I want to dedicate this book to a very special lady in my life, Kathy Evans. We have since gone on to be married on February 14,1997, in Olympia, Washington. Thank you Kathy for being your wonderful loving self. Your love and encouragement has the support that seen me through the daunting task of writing this book. You have made my life very happy and fulfilling. Our loving relationship remains like a rose. Very beautiful and delicate in appearance, but quite hardy with a great deal of strength. Forever my Love...

The Eye of the Tiger

◆

To enhance one's learning is to open the possibilities of the world to him. Also to enhance one's learning is as simple as helping the individual to focus and retain information for ready recall when it is needed. Possibly the most difficult challenge will be to clearly establish what triggers the individual's blocks.

There can be many blocks an individual can develop to memory retention and rapid recall of learned information. Stress is possibly the most widely recognized source of interference. For a number of people just the idea of sitting down to talk about a test brings the anxiety level up over the top. In order to effectively offer treatment the therapist must first help the patient clearly identify what is blocking them from retention and recall. This could be as simple as stress and anxiety to even short term memory loss induced by medications or physical trauma. Possibly the most effective method to sort out the root causes is to take the patient through a session of guided imagery and probe their feelings and thoughts leading up to the educational/testing situation.

In the fall of 1990 my youngest son, Marc, had expressed his concern about his ability to retain and recall information in his high school classes. His grade point average was a dismal 2.1. Marc had the desire to get better grades, but was reluctant to be seen doing much in public to work toward better grades. After all, image was extremely important in the high school setting if one is to be accepted by the majority of his peers. Marc was concerned if he was to outwardly apply himself to education in the high school setting he would have been most likely been labeled a nerd or geek. Image seems to be so crucial during those high school years and allows the teenager to make poor life decisions. At all age levels we see how peer pressure can be very devastating.

As a therapist I could immediately identify several areas that a hypnotic intervention could be helpful with. As with many parents, I had to fight the temptation of wanting Marc to conform to my "model of the world" when it comes to expectations and educational outcomes. This meant slowing down a bit and approaching him as an individual sixteen-year-old male to be communicated with, and not communicated at. As a therapist it is all to easy to get caught up in the trap of prescribing treatment when we do not have a clearly defined set of signs and symptoms surrounding the problem area. As a parent it becomes even easier at times to overlook the individuality of your own child as we often view them as an extension of ourselves.

With teenagers, as with many adults, they initially lack insight into their own problems, so they have much difficulty in providing an accurate in depth description of the existing problem. When interviewing with Marc I patiently waited while he talked his way through the blame frame in describing his problem. Once we got past the initial idea of the quality of teachers, peer group, and relevance of the material presented to apply to actual life skills, we could move on to the next level. At this point we discussed what Marc could do differently to get better grades. I feel it is important to allow your patients to fully move through the blame frame of the interview so that negative information can be aired out before trying to move ahead. The concept of blaming is nothing new; many people need to pass through this stage before being able to fully focus on their problems in a healthy and constructive manner. These issues in the blame frame should not be taken lightly. They have relevance in our education and socialization process.

From Marc's "model of the world" he saw his problem with not getting better grades as an inability to (1) focus on the information being presented by the teachers and (2) not being able to readily retrieve the needed information during class time for tests and discussions. First we discussed in great detail what Marc felt was getting in his way of being able to focus on the information being presented by the teacher. After sifting through many generalities we mutually concluded that most of the information being put forth by his teachers had no day-to-day practical application in the real world; therefore, Marc could not generate any interest in most of the material being presented in the classroom. For Marc, no relevance to his life equaled no interest to learn and retain information in the classroom. Secondly we discussed what was happening when he could not call information up from his memory when the information was needed for testing. After carefully sorting out all this information we arrived at a mutual conclusion.

Self-image emerged as the biggest culprit. The information Marc needed was in his memory, but a lack of self-confidence was clearly interfering with his ability to recall information on demand. This coupled with the stress factor of taking tests was clearly debilitating. Self-confidence and stress seemed to be the major issues shaping up.

Now Marc's treatment outcomes were starting to take a clear shape. The big lever of success in Marc attaining meaningful change comes from the fact that he was instrumental in the discovery phase and planning of his treatment. Whenever a person's outcomes are self directed the possibility of success increases three fold. The treatment strategy for Marc was developed and integrated into a three-point plan. First was for Marc to be able to develop a strong and eager interest in the information being provided in the classroom. Secondly he was to improve his ability for recall through strengthening his self-image and trusting himself. By trusting himself, Marc would be much more confident in his abilities to apply his learned information. Thirdly we went back to his "blame frame" to look at the issue of peer pressure to conform to one group or another for acceptance. Normally it is advisable to only tackle one issue per trance for the maximum effectiveness. In Marc's situation I was able to deal with all three issue during the same trance. This was feasible because all three issues had the same common denominator of self-image. Whenever you can establish a common thread with multiple issues it is possible to be highly successfully addressed in the same trance due to the continuity between issues. Care must be taken to ensure that you maintain that common thread through out the trance session to successfully address all treatment issues. I recommend that you exercise through planning before attempting to address multiple issues in the same trance session.

The first trance session with Marc was aimed at mainly sensitizing him to trance work. In this particular case I had to be very careful to not let the trance work become a power struggle between parent and child. I began by letting Marc choose how he wanted to position himself, he choose to lie on the couch to start with. Then I asked him to pick out any object in his line of sight to look at. With Marc lying down everything in his field of vision was well above his line of sight. To this point everything about the trance work was within his control. I have found that with most patients, even relatives, that control issues can develop very easily when trying to do trance work. With the beginning of initial trance work people have related to me that they have had an underlying fear of being out of control. Usually after the first trance session their fear are alleviated and they can become deeply involved in trance work. As I had stated earlier this session was aimed at sensitizing Marc to state of hypnotic trance. Marc went into trance with a great deal of ease and no apparent apprehension. I took him in and out of trance three different times. Each time I started the induction with eye fixation and simply paced his breathing with my patter of soothing and relaxing terms as he went deeper with each induction. With this induction, as with all my inductions for my patients I refuse to let the speed of the induction become an issue for me, quality before the speed of quantity.

For Marc's second session we only waited three days before picking back up with trance work. In this session Marc went into trance very quickly and easily. I believe he was in the state of somnambulism within three minutes! What I established first for Marc was the same thing I do for all my patients. I had him create his special place in his mind's eye and develop a clear and wonderful picture of it. I use the concept of developing a special place as a fail safe in the event that if something negative arises during trance the patient will have a safe and calm place to move their mind to. Also the special place sets up the building blocks for teaching the patient how to use guided imagery for their own relaxation and possibly self-hypnosis. In this second session I developed a metaphor for Marc that addressed his treatment goals. This metaphor I have named "The Eye of the Tiger". A copy of this metaphor is added to the last page of this chapter.

Once Marc had developed his special place I slowly read the metaphor to him as I continued to pace his breathing pattern. After the metaphor I gave Marc a post hypnotic suggestion that whenever he found himself not able to recall learned information that he could simply touch his left index finger and thumb together. As his finger and thumb touched he would find himself smiling and greatly relaxing. This was aimed at giving him a tool to de-stress himself during the stress of test taking.

Marc's third session came only two days later at his request. He had found he really enjoyed the benefits of deep relaxation and his special place. Once again I repeated the metaphor and reinforced the post hypnotic suggestion for his stress relief. Approximately one week later Marc and I did a fourth and final session. I maintained the consistency of my approach to his trance work. The metaphor was applied first and then secondly his post-hypnotic suggestion was reinforced.

The follow up on this work did reveal an improvement in Marc's grade point level. His GPA had gone from 2.1% to a high of 3.6%. In review, the essence of success with this hypnotic intervention occurred by involving Marc in the treatment planning process right from the beginning. To prescribe his needs would have only set up a large amount of resentment and invoke some feelings of not being in control of his situation. This particular thought holds true whether you are working with adolescents or adults. Resentments set up resistance and only serve to validate their concern for being out of control and reinforce their low self-esteem.

Whenever possible I highly recommend that the patient take an active part in prescribing their own treatment. If the patient is active in the decision making process the likelihood of success is greatly increased due to the patient owning his own ideas about his treatment needs. Another issue that should not be overlooked is treating teenagers versus treating adults. Often the therapist tries to separate teens and adults in treatment planning. This more often than not will set up situations for resistance and various other problems. From about age fourteen and up I recommend approaching all patients the same in treatment planning.

Most everyone wants to have a say in their treatment planning. The following metaphor was used during the trance work. It is presented as double spaced and easy to use for your reference.

Eye of the Tiger

The script begins when a state of somnambulism is reached.

As you continue to relax deeply, picture yourself in the classroom at school, sitting where you usually sit. The teacher is talking, and you can see yourself listening. You see yourself listening closely, very intently on what the teacher is saying. Even more interesting is seeing how well focused you remain as the teacher is talking. Knowing now that no word will escape you, somewhere in all that is said is very, very important information that you must have. Seeing yourself now taking in every word and understanding with much wisdom all that is said. Able to concentrate and focus with the Eye of the Tiger. Focusing so sharply that no information can escape you. Much like the tiger that stalks his prey. Very focused and all the information comes to you with great ease. Just as you sit down to take a test in the classroom, notice that wonderful feeling of self-confidence well up inside of you. Focusing clearly, quickly and confidently on the questions before you. Much like the eye of the tiger as he stalks his prey. As you read the questions one at a time, notice a small smile start to come across your face as the information you need comes to you clearly from your memory. The information seems to come to you without any great effort or great concern. How very wonderful to be able to focus so clearly and easily without any strain. Know that as you look into the mirror you see a trusted friend there, yes, that's you in the mirror. You can see yourself looking just the way you want to look, feeling calm and confident in how you look. Knowing the whole while those other people's opinions are not really important to you any more. It is all right to just be yourself, not anyone else, being very pleased with yourself. It really is okay to be the kind of person you really want to be. Perhaps even others will have discovered this secret, a secret that not many people are fortunate to understand. That is to simply understand that it is all right to love yourself and find your own happiness and style. Just dare to be you, and only you, that wonderful person in the mirror that you see. That happy person looking just the way you want to look.

Raising Self Esteem

This is a long-standing problem for many people in our society. Take the patient to at least a medium state of trance and read the following script while pacing the patient's breathing. Reinforce in future sessions as needed.

Do you know of Beethoven, who became increasingly deaf as he got older, but kept on working, writing music that he could not hear, until one day, one evening, he conducted the symphony as they played his newest work, a concerto, and when it was finished the crowd erupted in applause, they stood and cheered, but he could not hear, he stood there facing the orchestra, unaware of the audience's approval until someone walked out and turned him around so he could see what he could not hear, only then did he know what everyone needs to know, but sometimes can't hear, like the woman I have heard of, black hair, black eyes, stocky build, a bright professional woman who hated herself and hated her life, she thought she was ugly and awful, and she thought that was why so many awful things had happened to her, but one day she was having lunch with a friend, an artist she had known for a time, and she said to her friend, that there were so many beautiful women, and they all seemed to be on that street that day, and her friend simply said, I think you're the most beautiful woman I've ever seen, and went on eating, as if it were nothing, and that simple observation, that simply statement of opinion, matter of fact, not flattery, wouldn't go away, couldn't be undone, her friend was an artist who knew what beauty was, so she could not ignore it, and she could not forget it, instead she begin to look at herself, each day in the mirror, and she began to look at others, how they looked, who they were with, and it was very hard and scary at first to realize how wrong she had been, how wrong her mother had been, how wrong she had been about herself in so many different ways, but over time she had began to accept it, she was not ugly, she was not stupid, she was not a bad person , she was attractive and likeable and nice, and she did not have to settle for less than she deserved, how she thought changed, how she felt changed, what she did changed, her life changed, all because of one brief comment, one brief glimpse of herself, a clear admission of something she had been unable to let herself know before, that truth is beauty and beauty truth, and the truth about oneself, one's beauty, is in the eye of the beholder, but what we hear is not always measured on a hearing test, Beethoven heard things in his mind that his ears could no longer hear, and many animals can hear sounds, that the human ear cannot, and all we ever need to hear is that there is nothing else we need to do, except hear the beauty of what is.

(Terminate Trance)

Surviving Abuse

———————— ◆ ————————

Abuse comes in many shapes and forms, emotional and physical in nature. Any time a human being is disrespected, manipulated, threatened, or physically struck they become victims of abuse. No one in our society seems to be immune to abuse and its aftermath. There are a countless number of people out there that are walking around with a great deal of unresolved issues from past abuse. It also seems that the majority of these people have not and will not seek assistance to address their unresolved issues until their life situation reaches a state of crisis. This helps set the scene for this chapter regarding an abuse victim.

The patient in this case was a thirty two year old divorced white male whom we shall call Bob to protect his real identity. He was referred by a friend for the treatment of depression. Bob's history shows that he had been married eleven years before his sought a divorce. They had two boys, ages seven and nine. He has held the same job with the federal government for the past fourteen years. Bob initially presented as a fairly well adjusted individual considering he was newly divorced. He complained of being plagued with depression for six or seven years. He went on to describe the symptoms of his depression as a loss of energy, feeling tired all the time, difficulty concentrating, and a low libido. Bob stated that his major concern was his loss of energy and feeling tired all the time. He went on to say that he had been seeing a psychiatrist for the past fifteen months without any acceptable change. The doctor had him on various anti-depressants and he felt he still was not able to elevate his energy level. A previous patient of mine that he was acquainted with had recommended he see me.

As standard procedure I attempted to probe Bob's background in search of a well-defined time of onset of his depression. It became apparent quickly that there seemed to be no conscious link that would recall the onset of his depression. I had Bob sign a release of information so I could obtain a summary of treatment from his psychiatrist. The psychiatrist surmised that Bob's depression centered around his dysfunctional marriage. Bob said he refused to accept the notion that his previous marriage was the main cause of his depression. He stated that he felt that there was something inside himself that he just could not get a handle on that may be the root link to his depression.

Bob stated that he had never been hypnotized before that he was aware of, but said that he would welcome the opportunity to experience trance. In Bob's second session with me I introduced him to the experience of hypnotic trance. Bob proved to be an excellent hypnotic subject as he slipped into a deep and comfortable state of trance, but he was unusually resistive to coming back out of trance during this first set of inductions. He explained his trance experience as a beautiful escape that he really was reluctant to leave. We made an appointment for his third session in one week.

For Bob's third session we started with developing a treatment approach before proceeding with more trance work. Since Bob was not able to establish any root cause for depression I felt we needed to pursue that issue more in depth. Taking into account that he was able to go very deeply into trance and then expressed a reluctance to leave trance left me suspecting he may have possible abuse issues from his past. Over the years I have noted that abuse victims always seemed to carry with them the ability to be very good escape artists. This is a learned skill that abuse victims seem to acquire to be able to survive in their situation. They have a very strong ability to detach themselves from reality and mentally retreat somewhere within their mind. I explained this to Bob and then asked him if hypnotically we could take a trip inside his mind in search of answers.

For this induction I asked Bob to just close his eyes and recall those wonderful feelings of trance that he had experienced the week before. During this time I kept reinforcing the trance until I was certain that Bob was in a state of somnambulism. I then instructed Bob to create his special place in his mind's eye. I told him he could add to or take away anything from his special place that he wanted. The intent was to develop a safe fall back situation and I asked him to see himself just as he wanted to be, comfortable, safe, and very much in control. As Bob continued to sit there enjoying his special place I asked him to let his mind wander back in time to that event in his life that he felt was the very worst, that time when he might have felt very sad so long ago. After about a minute of silence a few tears started to run down his face and his breathing quickened. I told Bob that he could remember what had made him so sad after he came out of trance. At that time I also told him to let his mind return to his special place. After a few minutes I brought Bob back out from trance to a full state of complete consciousness.

Trough a tearful conversation Bob explained that he had remembered that his father had sexually abused him at about age seven or eight. He described it as a terrible dream that just came floating back. I asked Bob to describe the feelings that he experienced in trance. Bob described those feelings as fear, feeling lost, betrayed, and that he was a bad person. He went on to say that he realized he had buried all this in his memory to try and avoid dealing with the emotional pain. I pointed out to Bob that his feelings in trance were not much different that the way he described his symptoms of depression. By the end of the session Bob was feeling better and appeared very stable. We scheduled his next appointment for five days from that date to continue therapy.

Upon Bob's return he reported that the memory of his father sexually abusing him was totally clear now. He said he felt very bad about all the episodes of sexual abuse, but said he did not know what to do with all this recovered information. We discussed his situation and talked about his options. There was nothing that could be done directly with his father as he had passed away seven years ago. I pointed out to Bob that his father's death seven years ago also correlates with him reporting his depression onset as seven years ago. Bob stated he did not want to try and just rebury this information or ignore it, but felt he had to do something positive with this information so he could feel better.

From this point we initiated a trance and he quickly returned to the state of somnambulism where we could work on his grieving of the past situation. To facilitate his grieving process I shared my metaphor "goodbye" with him in trance. At the end of this chapter you will find a copy of the metaphor titled "goodbye". During the trance I reinforced the concept of letting go of past feelings. After the trance session I gave Bob a homework project to work on before returning in one week. He was to write a letter to his father telling him how he feels, how he hurts, and if possible tell his father he forgives him.

The following week Bob returned as scheduled and he brought with him his letter to his father. Bob had spared no details in his letter as it was nearly six pages long. One unusual thing about his letter to his father was that he had not signed it! When I pointed this out to Bob he said he had not noticed that he failed to sign the letter. At some length we discussed why he had not signed the letter. I offered several possibilities from just forgetting to possibly avoiding taking responsibility and ownership for the letter. Bob decided that he must have been avoiding taking ownership for the letter to avoid future negative feelings. With that decision made I gave Bob an ink pen and asked him to sign the letter to complete the assignment. To take this a step further I had Bob read the letter out loud. Bob's voice was strained and broke several times as he was reading. Once he was done he asked me if he could read the letter again out loud. This time there was less strain in his voice and he sounded strong and confident. After that reading I told him I would become the eternal postmaster for his letter.

At that point we started trance work again. This time I repeated the metaphor and reinforced his self-esteem. Also in the trance I reinforced the idea with him that as a child he had no control over his situation, but now as an adult he does not need to see himself as a bad person as he is in complete control of his life. We agreed this would be his final session unless something else comes up unexpected.

Approximately six months later I did a telephone follow up with Bob. He reported that his depression seemed to be gone. He sounded very pleased with his increased level of energy now and reported going off his anti-depressant about two months after our last session. Bob also stated that he is not plagued with memories of his sexual abuse.

In summation, the subconscious rarely lets any issue be buried and forgotten for a lifetime. Somewhere, somehow, the old unresolved issues are destined to re-surface to be dealt with. As demonstrated with this case, age regression is not always needed to retrieve information from the past. With the patient being in trance this thing we call hyper-mensis will automatically increase the individual's memory by up to sixty five percent. This can occur easily in trance because all the daily chatter that goes on in the mind can be quieted and a clearer path to recall takes place.

The metaphorical scripts used during the trance work are presented double spaced in an easy to use format.

Saying Good-Bye

As you continue to relax and experience the awareness of many different things. You may begin to wonder how many different ways there are to heal a wound. A wound from long ago that never healed, but remained to change the way you think and feel. Like a woman I know who always wondered why she was the way she was. Until one day she discovered a child within. A sad child, an unhappy child, an angry hurt child from long ago. A child she always heard in the background. A child she protected and did everything for today. A child who made her feel so sad, and she would do anything to keep that child quiet, to keep that child happy. To give that child what it wanted and needed. When I asked her what needed to be done she said she needed to say goodbye to that child. And she needed to hug that child, to hold that child, and to tell that child how very, very sorry she was for those things that had happened to it. She felt so badly for the pain, so badly for the fear, so badly for the anger, but she knew she had to say goodbye. Finally she had to leave it behind and go on with her life. She knew there was nothing she could do to save that child. She was not able to change the past, to undo what was, and there was nothing more she could do. So she hugged the child and said goodbye and walked away, very far away, and she cried and cried. The hardest thing she had ever done was to say goodbye, leave it behind, and abandon it to the past. She felt awful, but she knew what had to be done. All she could do was watch the child slowly disappear; there was nothing she could do to change the past. It was beyond her control now, as it was now in the past. Nothing she could do to undo what the child went through, but afterwards she was free, felt free to do what she wanted. The child was gone and she was free, free of the past, free to be, so as you continue to relax. Continue to drift down, your unconscious mind knows what you can do or not do. You can feel the freedom of that letting go in your own way, even as you drift more deeply your unconscious mind will take all of this knowledge and put it in good order for you.

Meeting the Inner Child

The purpose of this exercise is to assist the patient in getting in touch with his inner child. This in itself should generate insight for the patients as to what his present needs might be and lend additional insight into life long behaviors.

Take client down in trance to a medium state.

Tell the patient the following story, pacing his breathing throughout trance.

Think back now to when you were 7 or 8 years old, (Pause) now picture in your mind the place you lived when you were that age, (Pause) now imagine that you are standing outside that very place looking at it, now walk around to the door you mainly used when you were a child, slowly now open the door and walk in, notice the sights, sounds and smells that were familiar to you (Pause), continue to walk to the room where you used to feel the most secure and comfortable in there as that 7 or 8 year old child, notice what you are doing, how were you dressed? (Pause) Now tell the child the most important/valuable information that he or she can use in his coming years now that you are an adult and have lived those years (Pause). Go ahead now and speak to the child and tell him what he needs to know (Pause). Now give the child a hug before you leave, if you can't hug the child, and then just say good-bye (Pause). Now turn and walk back out the same way you came in. Continue to walk to the location where you first viewed the place where you lived (Terminate trance, ensuring that you empower the client's memory).

You can expect this experience to be very impactful and profound for some clients. You need to ask your clients to explain their experience in detail to you from start to finish. This experience should help build insight and possibly identify issues to be resolved in the future.

Adults with Abusive Childhood Issues

Application: For those patients still bothered by childhood abuse issues, physical, emotional and sexual.

Move the patient down in trance to a medium state, read the following script slowly as you continue to pace the client's breathing throughout trance.

You know, and I know, that nothing can undo what happened to you in the past, what was to you was done to you back then, but that was then, and this is now, you can stop the pain and fear, you can put an end to it, now, and you already know how, you know how to forget to pay attention to particular things, you know how to shut doors and windows on the past, you know how to see things now for what they are now, not what was, and your unconscious knows how to walk forward in time across that line, a boundary line that marks a new beginning, that lets you join the present, as you let go of the past, that lets you see a future, when you will remember how good it felt today to let go of that past, to say goodbye to it, and to let yourself feel okay, so go ahead now and keep going ahead later on, because that past is through and you are just you here and now, and when you get home, there is something you can do to put this away and get on with the future, some way for you, a ritual perhaps, a ceremonial letting go, throwing something away to let yourself know that the past is done and the future has begun, and you will do that, will you not?

(Terminate trance)

The Eagle Eye of Sports Performance

◆

Some of the key elements to excelling in sports are a high degree of focus and conditioned reflex. Through the use of hypnosis the key elements and many more can be enhanced in a short period of time. This procedure became quite popular in the 1980's, but most people refer to it as guided imagery. A goodly number of people fail to excel at sports because that cannot honestly see themselves doing the sporting function successfully. Secondly, people are generally plagued with overactive minds, unable to focus because some many different thoughts keep interrupting their concentration. By intervening hypnotically and strengthen the individual's concentration and ego strength, positive results can occur rapidly. Before an effective intervention can take place, it is necessary for the individual to have fairly comprehensive understanding of the sport he is pursuing. The understanding needs to be specifically in the form of the required movement, actions and objectives.

The following case is about a young man who was a high school football player we will call Troy for the sake of confidentiality. Troy described his problem with football as being unable to react fast enough to football situations as they developed on the playing field. His job on the football team was to be a defensive linebacker and stop the offensive ball carrier. Troy went on to explain this problem more specifically as being unable to keep track of who had the ball and which way they were going with it. He described feeling like he was in slow motion all the time during the football game. He felt he was about only fifty percent effective on the football team. I gave Troy a short series of tests to measure his hand-eye coordination and his ability to concentrate.

The results of these tests were quite average, very much in the normal range for an adolescent. Physically he appeared quite fit and healthy. His ego strength seemed typically wobbly for an adolescent. Troy's ego state and support systems seemed to be something that would bear further investigation. He reported that he felt his parents were too restrictive and rarely attended any of the football games he participated in. He had a sister that he described as a bookworm. Troy described his high school years up to this point as about average. He did appear to be socializing well and developing relationships in school. His grade point average for the last school quarter was 3.1 percent. The majority of his background sounded average for his adolescent years. Before the initial session was concluded I took Troy down in trance to start sensitizing him to hypnosis. As with most teenage subjects he was an excellent hypnotic subject. I made an appointment for him to return in four days for his next session.

Troy showed for his next appointment as scheduled. He appeared quite relaxed and was looking forward to more trance work. Using the eye fixation technique, I asked him to focus his gaze at an object above eye level. I took him down into trance to a good working state of somnambulism to start the intervention. During the induction I also had Troy create a special place for himself in trance as a fall back position. First we started with using the metaphor "Sports Safe". From that metaphor I switched to talking to Troy about being on the football field, telling him that he could see himself there looking just the way he wanted to be and imagining that his vision was as sharp and clear as that of an eagle searching for its prey. With this focus he could clearly see the football being snapped and the quarterback handing the ball off as he effortlessly tracked the ball carrier and tackles him. I instructed Troy to imagine how he felt after executing such a perfect play, paying special attention to those wonderful feelings and enjoy them. Now once again I took Troy through the process of tracking the ball carrier with the eye of an eagle and then capturing his prey. During this session the eye of the eagle was reinforced three times. Before bring him up from trance I asked him to rehearse this scene in his mind several times over until it became a smooth and effortless flow.

Debriefing Troy after the trance session, he reported feeling very confident and relaxed. He said he could clearly recall the scene of himself on the football field doing his job perfectly. He had a football game Friday evening so I scheduled him to return and see me the following Monday. Whatever the results of the Friday football game I stressed to Troy to continue to repeat this football imagery we had developed.

Troy returned on Monday as scheduled with a big grin on his face. He described his performance in the Friday football game as awesome. He said the coach and other members of the football team had congratulated him on how his game was improving. Troy explained that when he ran out onto the football field at the start of the game he keep reminding himself of the eye of the eagle. We talked at great length about the various plays that he executed on the playing field and that wonderful feeling that he got after each successful play.

By linking positive feelings to positive behaviors it serves to better imprint and retain these more positive behaviors for a greater length of time. For this session we reinforced what he had already done in the previous session. This serves as another means for reinforcing the desired positive behavior. Troy had another football game coming up on Friday, so we scheduled him to return on Monday to get a better measure of his progress. During the week he was to continue to rehearse his football plays in his mind and maintain his eye of the eagle.

The following Monday Troy reported the same positive results as he had on Friday. He was just beaming with a very healthy ego. We talked about his improved performance and decided that we would not schedule a follow up appointment. Troy did state that he felt a little guilty, like he was cheating some how by using hypnosis to improve his game. I assured him that he was not cheating or violating any ethics by using hypnosis to improve his sports performance. I understand that all professional sports team use a similar approach for their players and they label it as guided imagery instead of hypnosis.

There seem to be various parts of an individual's personality that will hinder their sports performance. The ego I feel is the biggest culprit for most people. Also a good number of people have difficulty focusing intently for any length of time without other thoughts intruding or negative self talks starting. Another important item is that if a person can visualize himself doing something then he is capable of accomplishing it. If the individual cannot visualize himself doing something sporting in a successful manner that they may want to consider pursuing another form of entertainment. To attempt to assist someone to excel at baseball when he cannot visualize himself playing baseball would be much like trying to help a blind person hit a fastball with a bat.

The following metaphoric script is offered as an example of an intervention to improve sports performance. The metaphor is presented as double spaced in an easy to use format.

Sports Safe Script

Because everyone needs to relax at times, even Olympic athletes who are under great pressure to perform and be perfect in order to win. These winners need some ways to also relax and to put everything into perspective. To recognize that is just a sport and not a war between nations, a war represents pain and loss; a sport should represent a test of skill and entertainment. In this atomic age where a war could mean the end of life as we know it, we cannot afford to make even the smallest of mistakes. Some people are terrified that the fail-safe system will fail and that will be the end of the world. All because of some tiny mistake, somebody doing or saying something at the wrong time in the wrong place. This is where mistake cannot happen and it is comforting to note that almost everyplace else and error is just an opportunity to do it differently the next time. There will be a next time to do it even better than before. Perfection is rarely required and perfection is seldom needed. Even the Olympic athletes are never perfect all the time and sometimes do things wrong. When the Navaho Indians weave a rug they always leave a knot, an imperfection so the gods won't be angry with them trying to be as perfect as the gods. That is another story for another time. Think about what is really important and what is not, and how it could feel to give yourself permission to enjoy the feelings of the freedom to feel safe doing these things. Knowing that the world won't end if you leave a knot some place, so the gods can relax knowing you are not challenging them, just simply doing the best you can and letting it go at that.

Improving Sports Performance

This intervention is geared to assist the athlete in improving their performance in their chosen sport.

Start the intervention in the medium state and continue pacing the patient's breathing pattern.

Imagine preparing yourself for the challenge, your equipment is good and is adjusted to your needs, you are prepared both physically and mentally, now just imagine for a moment stressful situations that may arise...such as the weather, the actions of another player, or field conditions, and see yourself react to these conditions in a cool, undisturbed way. Now review in your mind your entire game (or sport) from start to finish, see it in slow motion...see it in as much detail as you can. Review all the strategy you used...this perfect game, your perfect game, can be played again and again, imagine yourself reaching your goal; you have reached your goal. You have reached this goal and you can go on to other goals whenever you like. Now just imagine how you felt during your perfect game, imagine that confidence and ease, you were focused and strong; imagine yourself begin again, take a few deep breaths and in slow motion see every action, feel every move in the most positive way…see yourself act and react, move perfectly, every muscle in harmony with your thought, see your strategy, see yourself moving perfectly, see every perfect move, and now notice how you feel, you feel relaxed, at ease, strong, alert, and clear-minded, your vision is sharp, your reflects are perfect, you feel great, now see yourself conclude and win the challenge, you feel pleased with yourself, and every correct move, every play is imprinted into your subconscious so that you can repeat your perfect game over and over like a film, now go back and once again replay the sequence in your mind, and this time at normal speed, imagine the sequence from start to finish…and see it in great detail, in the greatest of detail, imagine making all the right moves and playing a terrific game, the best game you ever played.

Self-Acceptance Intervention

This script is good for patients to learn and accept their own uniqueness as an individual.

Take the patient down in trance to a medium state and begin reading the script as you continue pacing their breathing.

As you have already guessed, there is no perfect way to relax or to enter into trance, because it happens naturally, it is always different each time, no two snowflakes are exactly alike, and even the fingerprints of twins differ, so who's to say which one is the right one, and which one is the left, and so no matter how hard we try to do things perfectly, the odd thing is we always prefer the thing that is different and unique, something that is one of a kind, like stamps printed upside down, or coins made a little bit wrong, those become prized collector's items, just because they are different from all the rest, even if you need a magnifying lens to see the imperfection, because we want to see things differently, to see things bigger or smaller than we think they are, like a mirror in a circus that changes our shape and form, so we can really see what different would be if different we really were, which may explain the collections in art museums around the world, on one wall is a Van Gogh, on another is a Picasso, their beauty and power stands out, but everything is out of place or out of proportion, two legs different lengths or two arms different sizes, and yet it is all art of the highest form, the different paintings, different styles, like clothing styles that change from one age to another, and yet each is beautiful and flattering in its own way, in the eye of the beholder every flower is unique, designed the way it should be to be exactly what it is, and that is why we used to play a game of sorts as children, to decide which flower we would be and which we already were, and then to really look at it later and be surprised by what we found, something you can do as well, whenever you decide which flower you belong to, but for right now we don't need to know how you will feel when you decide to know that what seems wrong can be quite right after all, after you do all your homework and explore your own museum in the gardens of your mind where you can collect what you need to know to protect your own treasure and to treasure what you have collected even after you think you know that you really do not know what they really think about what you think about you.

(Continue with intervention or terminate trance)

The Four of Us

———————————— ◆ ————————————

This case takes a look at multiple personalities from the hypnotic perspective. As time goes on more and more cases of multiple personalities are being documented by therapists around the world. The documentation I have seen reveals a very low success rate. In dealing with this problem we need to first realize that the majority of these patients are being maintained on psychotropic medications in conjunction with therapy. The most popular and well-known cases have been made into books and movies. Such as the "Three Faces of Eve" and "Sybil". With multiple personality patients there is theoretically no limit to the number of personalities one patient could have. With some patients it can be a very long and demanding task to document each personality that a patient might possess. As time goes on there seems to be an increasing number of multiple personalities being reported. This leads me to question with a certain amount of doubt the validity of some of these reported cases. I speculate that there might be a "fashionable" rush for some therapists to hurry up and "discover" a multiple personality case.

The following case is about a young lady who was referred to me from a colleague who was a former student of mine. The young lady we shall name Rita for the sake of confidentiality. Rita presented as a thirty one year old single Caucasian female employed as a teacher. She had been seeing my colleague for over a year and they had arrived at a point where there was no forward movement towards her treatment goals.

She reported being aware of the other personalities since about age seventeen. During her senior year in high school she reported that she first had the realization that she had multiple personalities. During her time in therapy she was able to document three additional personalities in conjunction to her base personality. During the previous time in therapy Rita and the therapist had searched in vain for a traumatic event that may have triggered the onset of her other personalities. At this point Rita seemed quite discouraged with therapy, yet was willing to continue to work on this problem.

Rita explained her other personalities to me in the order that they started emerging. At age seventeen she had begun experiencing Mary. Mary would emerge as the frightened little girl who sounded and behaved as if she were about seven or eight years old. Mary had a strong tendency to feel frightened of virtually everything in her environment and would spend most her time crying and weeping. Mary would frequently emerge while Rita was involved in intimate relationships. Rita explained that she now avoids intimate relationships for fear that Mary will re-emerge and leave her feeling extremely vulnerable.

The second personality to emerge at about age nineteen was Heather. She describes Heather as simply a whore who would have sex with nearly any man that was available. Rita displayed a great deal of disgust and frustration while talking about Heather. She stated that Heather would only appear two or three times a year, act out and subside. Rita said that these past emergence of Heather had left her with a minor sexually transmitted disease to deal with. Rita stated that she felt her libido was about normal, except when Heather would appear.

The third personality to evolve was Mandy at about age twenty-four. Rita described Mandy as an arrogant and very proper person. She equated Mandy to a very proper southern lady, much like the ladies in the movie "Gone with the Wind". At this time Rita had no real complaints about Mandy and her behavior. She went on to explain that Mandy's behavior seemed quite safe compared to her other alternate personalities. Rita went on to explain that Mandy only surfaces maybe only once a year and may remain for five or six days and then subside.

Rita's three alternate personalities seemed to offer one another some balance. Heather was the wild one, Mandy was the very proper lady, and there was Mary who used as apparently a last resort for coping when the other personalities did not have the resources to deal with a given situation. The question still lingers, what was the catalysis that started generating these alternate personalities?

Rita's upbringing seemed quite average as she explained it. Her mother stayed at home and raised the children and her father was a minister in a small rural community. She had one brother that was two years older. He was an attorney and lived on the east coast. She said they were very close and talked often on the telephone. Rita's account of her school years seemed quite average, everything in her up bringing seemed almost picture perfect. The perfection of her growing up made me a little suspicious that she was not relating everything or had forgotten some areas of her teen years.

With the required release of information form signed by Rita, the other therapist furnished me a summary of treatment from the time she was being treated by him. The summary indicated that they had attempted age regression several times in search of a traumatic event in her past with no success. Our first session was spent reviewing information and I continued to probe for new and relevant information.

For Rita's second session we started a hypnotic search of her past in pursuit of more information about possible trauma that had been buried in her subconscious mind. She was a very good hypnotic subject as I had suspected. Almost anyone with a developed level of disassociation proves to be an excellent hypnotic subject and she was no exception. During the session I regressed her back to age seven and then talked her through her growing years up to age nineteen with no significant information uncovered. Prior to starting the regression I had

Rita create a special place that we could use as a fallback position in the event something horrible should erupt during the trance work.

The main point that I got from this session was a notable fear she displayed towards her father. After the trance work I inquired more about her fear of her father. She dismissed it as a little child's respect for her father. Her father had passed away when she was twenty-four years old. I found that at age twenty-four was the same time that Mandy first appeared. Rita went on to relate her relationship with her father as normal, very respectful and obedient toward him. Before she left the session I asked her to write me a story about her father and mother during her growing years and to bring it with her for her next session. I still had some grave concerns about her relationship with her father, but by asking her to write about both parents broadened the focus enough that she would not dwell on her father's memory and possibly generate some resentment toward therapy for implying something negative about her father.

When Rita returned the following week she had written the story I had requested about her parents during her growing years. She wrote the story from a third person historical perspective. She mentioned all the family members in her story but left out any direct reference to herself! Nowhere in her story had she mentioned herself or a little girl growing up. When I asked Rita why she had omitted herself from the story she was at a loss for an answer. At first she thought I was reading her story wrong, but after I read it aloud she then accepted the fact that she was nowhere in the story. This served to strengthen my assumption that something had happened in the family unit that facilitated her development of her multiple personalities. When I offered this idea to her she vehemently denied that her multiple personalities had anything to do with her relationship with anyone in her family, especially her father. I thought her direct reference to her father specifically was something important. I had not used the term of father when I was discussing the possible family dysfunction. The reference to her father appeared to be as a slipup from her unconscious mind.

Rita was visually distraught from her discussion about her family, but I went on to discuss the concept of using hypnosleep as a way to access her unconscious mind as a means to discover new information. Hypnosleep is the concept of attaching a trance state to her sleeping state and giving her the suggestion that she would remember her childhood in more vivid detail. Her suggestion would also incorporate the idea that she would recall pieces of this information in a dream state over the next seven days so she would not be subjected to being flooded with memories. After trance I would also instruct her to keep a dream journal when she woke up in the mornings.

As soon as I had eye closure in this trance session with Rita I had a surprise! Her alternate personality named Mary started to emerge. There she sat weeping and sobbing in a little girl voice asking me to stop, stop before it hurts anymore. I asked her, "Is Rita okay now?' and she said, "She's okay right now". With the induction gone I asked Mary to be calm and assured her that there was no reason to be afraid. I continued to talk in a soothing manner for a minute more and then Mary was able to stop her crying. I continued to assure her that there was nothing to fear, but that the truth would give her peace. I asked Mary's personality to rest and allow me to speak to Rita. Slowly Mary subsided and Rita returned in a matter of two or three minutes. I asked Rita to recall what she could of what had just occurred. All she could report was feeling very fearful and scared. I told her we would rest for now and resume our session next week. For next week's session I scheduled two hours to give myself ample time to perform hypnosleep.

To start this session with Rita I took a very casual approach so as to not alarm her or any of her alternate personalities. We talked briefly and the conversation converted to a trance induction. The post hypnotic suggest was used that when she heard the word "sleep" from the sound of my voice she would drift off into a comfortable and deep sleep immediately. I then brought her up from trance and using the post hypnotic suggestion for sleep, she immediately drifted off to a natural state of sleep. After she was fast asleep I painstakingly started attaching a trance to her sleep. I gave her the post hypnotic suggestion that her past would come back to her in bits and pieces in a dreamlike state while she slept and she would be able to recall the information when she awoke. Much to my surprise when I gave her the post hypnotic suggestion the first time her body tensed up and it appeared she was shaking her head to indicate "no". By the time I had related the suggestion a third time there was no physical response from her. Once the post hypnotic suggestion was administered I allowed Rita to sleep for a few minutes and then woke her up. Before leaving my office I reminded her to keep a dream log during the coming week.

When Rita returned next week she looked very tired. She related that she had not had a good night of sleep all week. She had found herself waking up every time she started to dream! It was apparent that some mechanism in her subconscious was trying to protect her from her dreams and the information she was seeking. To better facilitate her sleep I took her into trance and removed her post hypnotic suggestion about dreaming. Was that was done I asked her subconscious to recreate a dreamlike state and allow the dreams to come forward very easily and very safely. I continued to emphasize the dream state and that she was safe. Then her breathing escalated a few times during the trance as if she were experiencing something fearful. I reminded her that she was safe and secure and would be able to bring that information back from trance with her. As she was in a pseudo dream like state I would not attempt to engage her in a dialogue during this trance experience as it would be incongruent with the dream state.

After Rita had become fully awake from trance I starting questioning her about the dreams she had just experienced. At first she was hesitating to speak of her dream experience, looking some what bewildered and disbelieving of her experience. As she started to relate the dream I monitored her closely to see if any of her alternate personalities would emerge to rescue her. Fortunately none of these other personalities appeared during the session. Rita went on to describe her dream as seeing herself with her father in his church office. She thought she might have been seven or eight years old at the time. In a shaky and fearful tone she related that her father had taken his trousers off, taken her by the arm and told her to touch him and pet his penis. At that point of starting to see her touching her father the dream faded away. As she related this story she began sobbing and crying and then started to become mildly angry. I encouraged her to be angry, that she had a right to be angry. I asked her to say it out loud as if she were talking to her father. At the end of this session both Rita and I were feeling spent. Another interesting thing worthy of being noted was that none of Rita's alternate personalities emerged to rescue her! Rita said she felt so drained, but in a way relieved in the sense that she had finally learned what she had been repressing for so long.

Over the next three sessions Rita said good-bye to her three alternate personalities during trance. Each personality was dealt with, with respect and then dismissed as its function was no longer needed. Over the next month Rita was able to consciously recall more and more of the sexual abuse by her father. During the preceding three months we dealt with sexual abuse issues and Rita was able to make reasonable peace with herself and her memories. Just as important, Rita's three alternate personalities have never re-appeared! After a one year follow-up phone call Rita reported she was doing well and had no serious lingering problems. She was active in a support group for incest victims and seemed well motivated.

Different therapists have taken various approaches to treating multiple personality patients. Some therapists will search the past for trauma while others will attempt to isolate and deal with each personality separately. The following are metaphoric scripts that I used during the sessions with Rita. The metaphors are presented in a double spaced format for ease of use.

Merging Script

As you drift into trance, your mind drifts also. Like water from one place to another. Automatically and effortlessly flowing going the easiest way to the sea. When you fly above it you can see the path it takes. All the tiny creeks and streams that wind their way down the hills and down to the valleys below. This is where they flow into the river and thee river becomes larger. Gaining more and more from each new stream that joins it and the river becomes one very large river. It flows gently down stream towards the sea. It winds its way around mountains and surges through the plains as it gathers more and more strength from other streams and rivers along the way. Eventually it reaches the bay where it spreads throughout the delta and joins the power of the ocean. Now it becomes a part of that sea of life, a part of everything. While you continue to relax I would like to talk to all of you. To all the personalities that make up the whole person. A bunch of personalities together can be a marvelous forest, and one of you alone is just a tree in the middle of nowhere. When things join together they gain strength and protection from each other. It is a sign of the times, headlines in the newspaper each day describe the way small companies are forming large healthy companies by joining together. A merger of resources, several small banks announced a merger the other day and it was difficult to work out who would be in charge. Eventually they worked it out so that everyone was happy. Everyone was represented and each group had its say so that in a short time when they changed their signs they also changed all their labels. No one will ever know that things were not always that way. It will just seem to be the way it ought to be. Together as one, to be one, just like a special color that is several blends together to be a new color. A special color all it own in that painting, a portrait perhaps of a family. A group of people living as one. Where each has special abilities and each has a special purpose to serve. Sometimes they begin keeping secrets from each other and the world. When that happens they are brought together and told to tell each other those secrets that they all need to know. When a mother has a secret or a father has a secret, or brothers and sisters have secrets, they all had secrets from outsiders. The family begins to fall apart and each member loses something. They all need each other and they begin to be mean to each other. They need to tell each other they are very, very sorry. They need to come together, to cry together, to love together, to share their lives and strengths so they can have their portrait painted. They look like they belong together as one and the artist can merge the colors as the relief and relaxation of them all. Allow the minds to drift together, winding gently but surely toward the sea. Where each can see and feel secure feelings of belonging. Here and now, safe and sound, because things change as relaxation occurs. Openness provides a well deserved rest after the effort it took to overcome those problems and to join together as one.

Peaceful Void

This procedure is designed to help your patients find an inner peace within themselves. Start this script at a medium depth of trance.

Now clear your mind for this journey, imagining that you have inhaled a green cloud, and exhale a leaf falling gently...as you inhale, the rising green cloud floats higher and higher. as you exhale the leaf floats down gently...inhale the rising green cloud...and exhale the gentle falling leaf...if you cannot see the color, then visualize the word green, look at each letter, g—r—e—e—n. now see the entire word green. The word green now becomes the color green. Now gently glide green into your heart center. Let your heart center accept it and radiate green from it. Allow green to soak into your compassionate heart and make the exchange of love with green. Both become one at this time. Imagine a glowing green light in your heart center that will be with you during this time. Take a few moments now to feel and experience this calming, cooling and soothing green glow as it emanates from your heart center (Pause). Now acknowledge unfilled desires of illusions and fantasy regarding outside people, objects, or addictions. They are something you desire, transform these desires into thoughts. Sink the thoughts down into your chest. Move them out of your mind and into the lower part of your body. Make the thoughts reality in your being. Transform the thoughts into transparent particles and bursts of clear energy. Imagine your thoughts one by one transforming into nothingness, into the void. Feel this void in detail; see its shape, size, color, thickness, weight, taste, and smell, feel it again (Pause). Now take the green light of love that has been soaking in your heart center and use it to caress the void. Treat it kindly and affectionately, as you would the outside person or object. Outside material and objects and inside emotions may try from time to time to enter this void. Recognize their importance and gently let them know that the void is a place for nothing, and that they may pass through and vanish, and know they will not disturb the void. Draw the void close to you, hug it, stroke it lovingly, and gently welcome it into your body…Allow the void to float within you, it is your friend, it may feel awkward at first, that's okay, don't try to fill the space. Enjoy the emptiness and joy. Just let the void exist and become the love that embraces it. When you feel you have experienced all that is necessary for now, bring yourself back to a conscious state.

Stress Reduction Intervention

No doubt you will have numerous patients that this intervention will apply to as stress is a high profile problem in our society. Start this script when you have deepened the patient to the medium state.

Because you are now relaxed, let any feelings you have buried come up to the surface, examine those feelings, decide which ones you want to keep and which ones you want to discard…keep the ones you need right now, and cast away the others. It is all right for you to feel sad or depressed sometimes. It is your way of being good to yourself. Depression is a healing process so you can allow yourself to mourn or be sad and when you have completed the time of sadness, set yourself free. You are good to yourself and the time will soon be over for those feelings and you will feel free from them. You will feel free because you can accept or discard any feelings you are through with. They are yours, and you can let them come and go, come and go as you need them. Now relax, and continue to relax, and feel yourself relaxed with your feelings, and think of how you are a whole person with many feelings that make you whole and healthy, and if any unwanted outside pressure comes at you, you are surrounded by a shield that protects you from pressure. The shield will protect you from pressure. The shield prevents outside pressure from invading you. Pressure bounces off and away from you, bounces off and away. no matter where it comes from, or who sends it, it just bounces off and away. It bounces off and away. You feel fine because the shield protects you all day from stress and pressure. You go through your day feeling fine. You watch the stress bounce off and away. The more stress outside, the calmer you feel inside. the calmer you feel inside. You are a calm person and you are shielded from stress. You act in ways that make you feel good. You now have new responses to old sit-uations. This new response will make you feel strong and calm and free. Your days will be full of accomplishments, and you will be pleased with those accomplishments. You will feel good about yourself because you have new responses that are making your day more pleasant, you are calm and strong and free from stress. You are completely free from stress. You are free of all stress.

Full Circle Recovery

◆

This story deals with alcoholism treatment with clinical hypnosis as the main treatment modality. In this century alone there have been various treatment models used in treatment centers all over the country. Clinical hypnosis is no stranger to this malady of treatment modalities. What I see as the main roadblock for hypnosis as a treatment method is the problem is that no one hypnotic style of intervention is successful with all alcoholic patients. Therapists and our society continue to search for one treatment approach for all alcoholics. I want to be among the first to voice my objections to attempts to standardizing the treatment of alcoholism and drug addiction. When treatment becomes standardized the individual losses his identity and ceases to be dealt with as an individual with his own personal needs to be met. This is much like trying to force a square peg into a round hole! For the time being I will climb down from my soapbox and proceed with the rest of this story.

This case is about a fellow we shall call Mike to protect his identity. He was self-referred to see me due to his problem with alcoholism. Mike presented as a thirty-three years old married Caucasian male with two minor children. He was employed as an underground miner at a local copper mine in the area. While interviewing Mike it was revealed that he had a very strong family history of alcoholism on his father's side of the family. Mike also reported a history of alcoholic blackouts, increased tolerance to alcohol, and sneaking drinks. His father died four years ago of alcohol related death. Mike reported only drinking socially up until the age of twenty-eight. From that point his drinking escalated over the next five years. Twenty-four months ago Mike was court ordered to treatment for alcoholism after a drinking while driving arrest. He had successfully completed the outpatient treatment and all other legal requirements. He reports he has been attending Alcoholics Anonymous meetings every week.

Over the past thirty days Mike reported having drank to the point of intoxication on two different occasions. He describes the drinking incidents as losing control as he dwelled on the idea of tasting whiskey again and getting numb again. Another problem Mike reported was having dreams two to three times a week over the last two months. The dreams were always the same; he dreamt he was drinking and when he woke up he felt momentarily intoxicated.

Mike denied any problems with his relationships or current employment. He also denied being on any legal or illegal drugs. He stated his wife was very loving and supportive over the years as he fought his battles with alcoholism. Despite his embarrassment he reports that he still attends one or two A.A. meetings a week as his job schedule would allow. Mike presented as sincere about regaining and maintaining his sobriety despite being somewhat depressed about his situation.

Mike and I spent the remainder of the first session focusing on putting together a treatment plan for him. I kept the focus on his wants instead of his needs. If Mike started working on his wants first then his likelihood of success would increase dramatically. After much discussion Mike felt he wanted to first work on getting rid of his drinking dreams. This seemed to be a sensible approach considering he denied he has no urge to drink until the dreams started. There appeared to be a possibility that if the dreams could be resolved then the overwhelming urge to drink might disappear.

Based on my experience these alcohol dreams are an expression of the unconscious desire to drink. The logical approach in this case would be to address the subconscious part that controls Mike's alcohol drinking behavior and attempt to uncover the "payoff" for those urges. This would be the approach for the next session in three days. Before returning for his next appointment Mike was to keep a dream journal and record all possible information after awakening from those dreams. This should provide more accurate information on the frequency of these drinking dreams and try to establish similarities in these dreams and then investigate external links that may set the unconscious up to have these dreams.

Mike returned for his next appointment with his dream journal. The journal showed he had these drinking dreams for three consecutive nights just prior to returning here. All three drinking dreams showed him sitting by himself drinking whiskey and water at his mother in laws kitchen table until he was too drunk to walk. When I questioned him about his relationship with his mother-in-law he stated that she was a real nuisance for him. He reported that his mother-in-law would come over to their house three or four times a week smelling of liquor and often trying to bait him into an argument with her. He would then get very angry and retreat to avoid a senseless argument.

Mike had a sudden flash of insight as we were talking. He made a correlation between his drinking dreams and his mother-in-law! Since so much time had been taken up processing the drinking dreams and his mother-in-law there was little time left for hypnotic work. For the remaining few minutes of the session I put Mike into trance so he could experience the feelings and start to become sensitized to the feelings to facilitate trance work in the next session. Mike was a real natural for trance work. I found that almost all alcoholics and drug addicts are excellent subjects for trance work because they spent so much time in a disassociated state with their addiction. Mike was also instructed to maintain his dream journal until he returned for his next session.

Mike returned as scheduled with his dream journal as requested. Over the past week he reported having only one drinking dream. Mike also reported that he had four encounters with his alcoholic mother-in-law. Interesting enough the drinking dream occurred on the day he had not encountered his mother-in-law! At this point I explained to Mike what I planned to do with him in trance work. I explained that I would take him down into trance and attempt to negotiate with his subconscious part that controlled his dreaming ability. Mike was very receptive to the idea and added how much he had enjoyed the trance experience last week.

Once trance had begun I easily deepened Mike to a state of somnambulism. Then I asked Mike's conscious mind drift into his special place and relax maybe even watching a good TV program! Once I had separated the conscious from the subconscious I installed ideomotor signaling for a line of communication. He was to raise his left index finger once for "yes" and twice for "no". Now the time had come to ask Mike's subconscious part that controls his dreaming behavior to communicate with me. Access to that part came very easily. To my knowledge this procedure of accessing parts was first documented by the late great Virginia Satir. The payoff was established as the old signal response to handle situations beyond his control. The old response was to drink until he was intoxicated as demonstrated in his drinking dreams. His creative subconscious part furnished us with three new and better ways to handle situations without drinking. After all this was established I brought Mike back up from trance to the conscious state. Before Mike departed my office I was able to get him to agree to talk over these three new behaviors with his wife. Since dealing effectively with his wife's mother was part of his issue it was important to keep her informed and continue to enlist her support.

Mike was punctual keeping his appointment as scheduled. He reported no further drinking dreams. Mike and his wife had decided that when her mother showed up at their place under the influence, Mike would give her a piece of A.A. literature instead of entering into an argument with her. This would be the cue for Mike's wife to ask her mother to please check in for alcohol treatment somewhere. Over the course of the week they confronted his wife's mother three times! Each time she was confronted she became very angry and left. Mike reported that his mother-in-law returned a fourth time but she was sober and generally ignored him much to his delight! Mike also related that he and his wife were very pleased with the outcome so far. Mike appeared very pleased with himself and how he was handling his situations. He stated that he has had no strong desire to drink. During the session we worked on developing behaviors to fill the void of the absent drinking behavior. For the next four sessions we continued to reinforce this work. Jointly Mike and I decided that he was done here, but the door was always open for him to return if he felt the need,

This case reinforces the concept that the subconscious mind is the caretaker for the individual. In Mike's sobriety he learned new and more appropriate behaviors to deal more effectively with life. In the case of dealing with his mother-in-law he was handed a multi faceted issue. Mike could not separate himself entirely from his wife's mother and still have a good relationship with his wife. Secondly, as a recovering alcoholic he could not communicate honestly with his mother-in-law for fear of hurting his wife. This case could possibly be dissected even further, but the primary issues were addressed as the patient had assigned importance to them. This case could have gone in a variety of different directions in search of different outcomes, but I have always subscribed to the idea that patients need to establish their own outcomes, not the therapist. Far too often therapists will attempt to superimpose their ideas on what the patient should have for outcomes. More often than not this will result in many frustrated and failed outcomes, especially with the chemically dependent.

The following metaphors were used several times over with this patient. The metaphors are presented in a double spaced format for ease of use. The script about self-hypnosis would be a good script to put on a cassette tape for your patients.

Craving Again

This is a story about a person named Marsha. Wedding bells in Marsha's future were not something she was looking forward to. It wasn't because it wasn't her own wedding, it didn't matter who was getting married. It was going to be a big problem for her as she was newly recovered from active alcoholism. She was very frightened about her urges and wanting to drink. Whenever she would have an urge and a thought about how much fun it would be to have a drink, she began worrying. She would be consumed by the thought she would find herself drinking again. She really had that experience that people have whenever you want to change some kind of behavior. Finding yourself moving two steps forward and one-step backwards. Having doubts whenever you think about engaging in that new behavior. It was only a few days before she was going to face that difficult situation. Any person who is working on recovery knows that wedding receptions can be one of the most difficult tests. With everybody drinking and engaging in that behavior that you are trying to stop. Fear, concern and apprehension were written all over her face when I saw her that day. She had good reason to be apprehensive; the odds of her staying away from using alcohol were slim. She thought about drinking a lot. It didn't seem she had the resources to avoid the temptation since she was new to recovery. She was nothing like Jane who had just cancelled her scheduled appointment with me. Jane had a great deal more experience with sobriety than Marsha. Also a lot more confidence and with good reason. Some might have said she was a little cocky, but she had good reason to be confident of her ability to stay sober. She never really had urges and didn't have to go through the changes and struggles like Marsha had to do to stay sober. Jane was even so confident that she was able to go to parties and not even want to drink. That was such a positive sign to a lot of people because when you can be around users and not want to use it can be a good indication that she was in complete control. Marsha's reception and Jane's party were obviously going to be two very different experiences; I wish Marsha had some of Jane's self-confidence. She could have really used it, but she did not have it to use. For each time you make a mistake in a behavior change you will learn from that mistake. I'm sure there are many experiences that even if you don't consciously recall the times when you have made mistakes and failed at things, you have been able to learn from them. You can unconsciously know that and unconsciously recall those experiences. I also look forward to celebrating with Jane at being able to once again not relapse in a tough situation. If she chanced to keep her appointment at all next week, so I really was quite surprised when I got a chance to celebrate Marsha's successful reception and talk to Jane about her relapse. Perhaps you have some ideas as to how Marsha was able to use her situation in a useful way. Now Jane found that it was hard to do what she thought was so easy. I asked Marsha how she was able to have those feelings that were so scary to her and yet act in a way that was totally opposite of those feelings. Act in a way that was so useful to her, basically what she said was she was able to take those actions that are most useful. For her it was to seek out those people at the reception who were most supportive of not drinking or find herself intrigued with something else. Several people have come from another country and how interesting it was to learn about their culture. She said she had learned to use her fear and urges as a barometer that indicated that there were things she needed to change. So each time in the future that she was to have those fears or urges, that would be her signal that it was time to do some new things. Jane also experienced some learning too. Later that can become evident, balancing confidence with over confidence is important in any behavior. The athlete who has no confidence will never enter the race. The athlete who is over confident may not train hard enough. I'm not sure what Jane thought she had learned. Just as I imagine that you're not really sure exactly what you are going to be learning later about it. On a conscious level some learning's are pretty obvious, but unconsciously those applications can be used in many different ways. So you simply apply this unconscious learning's and perhaps delight yourself in how you are able to later surprise and maybe impress yourself in exactly how you are able to apply that.

Anxiety Script

It is recommended to use this metaphor for clients with panic attacks and general anxiety.

Take the client to at least a medium state of trance and tell this story as you continue to pace his breathing.

It has been suggested by a French physician that when babies are born, they should not be held upside down, in a cold, bright, noisy operating room, and spanked to make them cry, instead they should be born into a warm, quiet room with soft, gentle lights and put into a warm bath, because when they are treated that way, they open their eyes and look around, they seem amazed and happy, they even seem to smile, they lie there quietly relaxed, and they grow up to be happier and more secure, all because they were treated gently, protected and taken care of, not hurt or scared, but just allowed to be safe and quiet for a while, a natural way of doing things that seems to work out well, because almost all animals have their babies on warm spring nights when it is safe to be born, and the mother can take care of them, and help them get used to things, slowly and comfortably adjust to things, and learn how to keep things under control, they learn to hide quietly in the tall grass, how to remain very still, even when there is danger near, and they learn to play happily, secure in the awareness that someone is nearby, protecting them, calmly watching out for them, and as they get older and wiser, they seem to calm down themselves, and become more quiet inside and out, as they use everything they've learned, because even a brief moment can provide a lesson to be used to keep oneself calm and quiet inside, the way warm water can seep throughout, even though only a small corner rests gently in that warm bath where a new born child rests and smiles, with a warm glow of safe comfort.

Escalator Technique

The technique used in this script is excellent for being able to go deep into Self-Hypnosis. This would also be a good script to put on a cassette tape for your use. Practice is the key to your success with any of these Self-Hypnotic techniques listed in this book.

Take a comfortable position in your chair. Close your eyes and breathe deeply two or three times. Now that you are comfortable, you will listen closely to my voice and follow all the suggestions given. Your eyes are now closed, take another deep breath, hold it a few seconds, and let it out. Mentally say to yourself, relax deeply, relax deeply, the more you can relax, and the more you concentrate, the deeper you will go into hypnosis. Let all your muscles go as loose and limp as possible. To do this, start with your right leg, tighten the muscles first, make the leg rigid, and then let it relax from your toe right up to your hip. Then tighten the muscles of the left leg, let that leg relax from the toes up. Let the stomach and abdominal area relax, then your chest and breathing muscles. The muscles of your back can loosen...your shoulders and neck muscles relaxing. Often we have tension in these areas. Let all these muscles relax. Now your arms right down to your finder tips. Even your facial muscles will relax; relaxation is so pleasant and comfortable. Let go completely and enjoy the relaxation. All tension seems to drain away and you soon find a listlessness creeping over you, with a sense of comfort and well-being. As you relax more and more, you will slip deeper and deeper into hypnosis. Your arms and legs may develop a feeling of heaviness, or instead you find your whole body feeling very light, as though you are floating on a soft cloud. Allow yourself to experience any such sensation you are having for a minute. Just let yourself go and feel the sensation of floating, or heaviness, or any other sensation you are experiencing (Ten-second pause). Now listen to me and imagine that you are standing at the top of an escalator such as those found in stores. See the steps moving down in front of you, and you see the railings. I am going to count from ten to zero, as I start to count imagine that you are stepping on the escalator, standing there with your hands on the railing while the steps move down in front of you, taking you with them, if you prefer, you can imagine a staircase or an elevator instead. If you have any difficulty visualizing the escalator or staircase or elevator just the count its self will take you deeper and deeper (Slowly). Ten, now you step on and start going down, nine…eight…seven…six, going deeper and deeper with each count. Five…four…three, still deeper. Two…one…and zero. Now you step off at the bottom and you will continue to go deeper still with each breath you take, deeper and deeper with each breath. You are so relaxed and so comfortable. Let go still more, notice your breathing, probably it is now slower and you are breathing more from the bottom of your lungs, abdominal breathing, as you go deeper into hypnosis, my voice may seem to drift away from you as though it were coming from a great distance, but you shall continue to hear it and pay attention to the suggestions I shall make to you. You will be able to respond to these suggestions even though you are very relaxed and very comfortable (Slowly). Now you can imagine yourself to be strolling down the hall to a special room…a special room in your own mind…as you see yourself strolling down the hall, feeling fine, feeling pleasant and relaxed, you can indicate to yourself when you reach the room, you can have it any way you wish it to be. It can be large or small, light or dark, cool or warm, furnished in any way you wish so that it is pleasant, comfortable and attractive. Now, approaching the door to this special room, now seeing yourself opening the door, entering the room, and closing the door. You can arrange yourself in any position that is comfortable, sitting, lying down, or strolling about. As you see yourself in this situation, you can allow yourself to go deeper and deeper, into a very deep state of concentration, a very deep state of relaxation. You know that you can always return to this special room in your mind when you wish to do so. You will be able to learn to use these techniques and these procedures for your own benefit and your own welfare, so that you can learn to relax and rest more deeply, study and concentrate more deeply, and to gain more self-understanding and more self-control. As you continue to use self-hypnosis, you are going to gain more self-confidence in your ability to accomplish your purposes. You will find that you are able to follow the suggestions you make to yourself in the trance state. You will find yourself able to go quickly into the trance state whenever you wish to do so, to go into hypnosis, all you have to do is close your eyes, make yourself comfortable, and drift into hypnosis. Some times it may help to think to yourself the phrase, "Now I am going into hypnosis", and repeat to yourself the words, "Relax deeply, relax deeply, relax deeply," saying them very slowly. As you do this you will slip off into hypnosis. You say nothing aloud, you merely think these words. When you have do this, take another deep breath to help you relax more and go through the relaxation just as you have done before. Tell your muscles to relax, as I have done. When you have finally relaxed your arms, imagine the escalator, elevator or staircase. Now you should count backwards from ten to zero, including the zero, count slowly. When ever you are ready to awaken all you need to do is think to yourself, "Now I am going to wake up". Then count slowly to five and you will be wide-awake. You will always awaken refreshed, relaxed and feeling fine. While you are in hypnosis, if something should happen so that you awaken, you do so instantly and spontaneously...something such as a phone ringing or a real emergency like a fire, you will awaken instantly and be wide awake and fully alert. Actually this would happen without such a suggestion being necessary, because your subconscious mind always protects you. Now you are resting comfortably, and you are in a hypnotic trance. Now let yourself experience deeper and deeper into the trance. Just pay attention to your breathing, notice how deep and regular your breathing is, you can go deeper into hypnosis with each breath you take, let each breath carry you deeper and deeper and deeper. Just like going to sleep except that you will keep hearing my voice and following my instructions. Now, continue to go deeper into hypnosis, to become more and more comfortable with each breath that you take. Breathing rhythmically and deeply, going deeper with each breath, let yourself go completely now, deeper and deeper, now that you are deeply relaxed, I want you to remain that way for a few minutes while you have an interesting and pleasant experience. I will not tell you what to experience, you can have the kind of experience that you choose to have, it may be a surprise to you, it may be a feeling or a memory, or a thought, you just let yourself experience it and enjoy it. As you have this experience you can go deeper and deeper into hypnosis. Now take a few minutes to let yourself experience whatever happens (three to four minute pause). In a few moments you will be able to complete the thought, feeling or memory. Now imagine that you are standing at the top of an escalator again. See the steps moving down in front of you, and see the railings. I am going to count from ten to zero, as I start to count, imagine that you are stepping on to the escalator, standing there with your hands on the railings while the steps move down in front of you, taking you with them. Ten...now you step on and start going down, nine...eight...seven...six...going deeper and deeper with each count, five...four...three.... still deeper, two...one...and zero. Now you step off at the bottom and will continue to go deeper and deeper with each breath you take, deeper and deeper with each breath, you are so relaxed and so comfortable. Let go still more. Now I want you to make a suggestion to yourself that you want to carry out. You can stay in a trance while you decide what suggestion you want to make, deciding will be easy, and it also will be easy for you to follow the suggestion whenever you wish to complete it. Go ahead now, and make your suggestion. Take whatever time you need, and after you have made your suggestion, you may arouse yourself from the trance at any time you wish and be wide awake and alert. You will be able to practice these techniques whenever you wish to do so, and you can learn to use them for your own benefit and your own welfare, so that you can become the kind of person you wish to be, the kind of person you can be.

Hungry For?

———————— ◆ ————————

This case takes us back to 1987 in Aurora, Colorado. I received this patient on referral from a former student of mine in the local area. He had been working with her for weight loss over the past two months with very limited success.

The patient presented as a thirty one year old divorced white female who was a college student with two young children. For the sake of confidentiality we will call her Sandy. Her desire was to lose thirty-one pounds and be able maintain her weight at one hundred and thirty pounds. For her height and body structure this outcome appeared reasonable. The patient stood five foot five inches tall with a medium bone structure. She had been seen by a medical doctor and physiological problems were ruled out. The doctor had put her on a two thousand calorie a day diet that she was never able to adhere to.

Other important information was that she has been divorced for two years and reported continued celibacy. After each child was born she was able to return to her normal weight without any problems. It was shortly after the divorce that she begun as steady weight gain. She had a bachelor's degree in business administration and was currently attending the state university to complete a master's program in business administration. When Sandy was referred to me she had only three months left to go before graduating from school. She reported having a large support network of other single mothers that were also attending school. She presented as a very goal oriented, analytical, and with a pleasant personality.

The hypnotherapist who referred Sandy to me had also forwarded a treatment summary of her time in treatment along with a signed release of information. The main approach in the past had been with behavior modification and with direct post hypnotic suggestions in an attempt to achieve weight loss. The patient expressed a reasonable concern about losing weight and being able to maintain at her goal weight. She went on to explain to me that she also had been practicing self-hypnosis in an attempt to lose weight and relax. Her weight loss over the past two months had never exceeded two pounds without gaining it right back.

Much to my delight Sandy was an excellent hypnotic subject! Just talking about the feelings associated with trance she would immediately enter into trance. Most of this initial session was spent with gather information from her, coupled with one quick trance induction. I was able to take her to a good working state of somnambulism in only a few minutes. Before Sandy departed my office I asked her to bring an object with her to the next session that represented the real her. With the homework assignment in place she was scheduled to return in three days.

Upon Sandy's return she brought with her a small teddy bear that she had since she was a small child. The teddy bear was obviously old and getting somewhat tattered. She explained that the bear had been the only constant in her growing years. The tears began to well up in her eyes as she explained that she could hold her teddy bear and love it without any bad feelings, for the teddy bear didn't expect anything from her.

For this trance session I took her down to the state of somnambulism and shared a metaphor with her that I had designed prior to her return. The metaphor was about a young princess named Ydnas (Sandy spelled backwards). In the metaphor the princess walked around a small pool of still water that was lined with beautiful flowers. In the pool of still water she saw her reflection in the water. She was looking just as beautiful as she wanted to be. The metaphor went on for about ten minutes directed at building her self-esteem. Before the trance session was concluded she was left with the suggestion that she would only eat three times a day at the same times she fed her children. Then I brought her up from trance temporarily and then re-induced trance. At this time I left her with the suggestion that her metabolism would remain the same twenty-four hours a day. This would allow her to burn off those extra calories even while she slept. One interesting reaction during the trance that merits a comment was when I pronounced her name backwards (Ydnas), she smiled slightly. I interpreted that as her subconscious recognition of her name. After trance she could not consciously recall the name of the princess in the metaphor. Her next appointment was scheduled in one week.

Upon Sandy's return for her third visit she reported that she had actually gained two pounds in one week! She reported that she had caught herself eating a few times between meals. Sandy also stated that her appetite seemed enormous over the past week. She explained that on several occasions she found herself eating without any conscious thought of eating. We talked further about all the other areas of her life were doing, school, kids, finances, etc. She reported that everything in her life was very stable and safe in her life. It was becoming obvious that there was something in her subconscious that was getting in the way of her meeting her goals. Since there were no apparent conscious clues available I felt that the subconscious held the answer. The most obvious clue about the subconscious was its rebellion over the past week with the gain of two pounds in one week.

For this trance session Sandy was deepened to the state of somnambulism and I immediately went to work probing the subconscious. I separated her conscious from her subconscious mind by asking her conscious mind to go to her special place she had created in earlier session. This would reduce any interference from her conscious mind. At first I could find no subconscious part that would take responsibility for

Sandy's weight loss or gain. No subconscious part could be identified that would be in conflict with her goal of losing weight. During this trance session I also reinforced her self-esteem. Before bring her back up from trance I left her with this post hypnotic suggestion: Some time during this coming week you will discover what you need to do to start losing weight, you might be asleep, you might be at home or at school when the answer you are searching for become clear. She was again scheduled to return here in one week for her next session. I felt relatively sure that if she had a conscious understanding of the road block to her weight loss she would make great strides with her high degree of goal orientation.

Four days later I received an excited phone call from Sandy who wanted to see me right away as she had discover some information about her weight problem. Fortunately I had a cancellation for that afternoon and was able to fit her in. When Sandy arrived she was still bubbling with a happy attitude as she explained to me what happened to her. She stated that two evening ago she was sitting at her kitchen table writing some paper for school when she remembered that the book she needed was in her book bag in her bedroom. She got up from the table and started to her bedroom when she found herself standing in front of the refrigerator with the door open looking for something to eat! At was at that point she had the revelation that she was subconsciously avoiding her bedroom, as the bedroom represented to her the absent relationship with a male and the sex life that would surely accompany it. Sandy estimated that she had been celibate for approximately two years now.

With this revelation we were now able to deal directly with the root cause of the problem. Sandy admitted that she wanted to be in a relationship and sexually active, but was afraid that the relationship would upset her lifestyle with her children and educational goals. Her divorce was also quite painful, as she had left an abusive relationship. Sandy immediately decided she would take a risk and start some kind of social

life with men. She was feeling bold enough at the moment to ask a fellow out for coffee that was in one of her classes that she was attracted to.
Sandy had also decided she wanted to continue on work on her self
esteem hypnotically. She felt also by remaining here in treatment that
she would have a safe support system as she ventured back into experiencing relationships.

For the next three months I saw Sandy every other week to reinforce
her self-esteem and continue to monitor her weight loss and be a safe
sounding board as she made healthy progress with male relationships.
Over this three months Sandy had lost fourteen pounds with little effort
and appeared to have no problem maintaining her weight loss. During
our trance work I reinforced her self-esteem and reassured her that she
was in control of her life and her relationships.

For stress reduction I gave Sandy the post hypnotic suggestion that
whenever she was feeling nervous and stressed all she had to do was
press her right thumb and index finger together to recall those beautiful
feelings of relaxation that she had experienced in trance and she would
immediately calm down.

After we concluded treatment I did a telephonic follow up with
Sandy and found that she had reached her target weight and was having
no problem maintaining her weight. She also happily reported that she
was now involved in an ongoing relation with a man and felt quite
secure and in control of her life.

In conclusion the main lesson learned here is a reinforcement of the
fact that usually weight loss usually goes beyond just simply shedding
pounds. It has been my experience that weight loss patients usually have
strong underlying issues that must be dealt with first before any successful weight loss can occur. A good many of these patients are not consciously aware of any underlying issues that drive their current weight
problem. The following metaphoric scripts are offered as an example of
interventions appropriate for this type of case. The metaphor titled

"View of Life" is aimed at helping the patient develop insight into their weight problem.

Balloons Galore

As you enjoy your special place in trance, knowing that you are comfortable and feeling so very good as you relax, enjoy and continue with observing the colors all about your special place. How very nice, notice all the other things about your special place. The sights, sounds, and the colors. No one else can be in your special place unless you allow them. What a wonderful place to be, so very comfortable and safe in your special place. Notice how you feel at this moment, so comfortable and safe. Notice that your (right) (left) hand you are holding three balloons, three of the ugliest balloons you have ever seen in your entire life. These ugly balloons look so out of place in your special place, these are very ugly, repulsive colors on these balloons. The first balloon has the words printed on it "craving sweets," wrote on the side, the words are clear and easy to read. The second ugly balloon has the words "light headiness" clearly printed on the side. The third ugly balloon has the word anxiety printed clearly on its side. You can see yourself standing there holding these three ugly balloons with the words, "craving sweets", "light headedness", and "anxiety" wrote on the balloons. These ugly balloons certainly do not belong in your special place. As you observe these ugly balloons with the words on them, you realize even more that they don't belong in your special place. When you are ready you can release these ugly balloons and watch them slowly float up and away, moving very slowly out of sight. As the balloons start to fade away in the distance, so do the words printed on them. Remembering briefly that the words were "craving sweets", "light headedness", and "anxiety". Watch them slowly disappear from sight. Now you can see yourself in your special place, free of the ugly balloons. Free of the craving of sweets, free of the light headedness and free of the anxiety. Seeing yourself in your special place looking slender, notice how you look now. How wonderful, notice how very wonderful you feel about yourself. Feeling so proud of yourself now that you are slender. How wonderful to be so rightfully proud of yourself, seeing yourself as slender. Experiencing how it feels to be slender, what a wonderful feeling as you continue to relax and go deeper.

A note on this using this metaphor. Change the words on the balloons to match the concerns of your patient. Different people will report various negative feelings and concerns about losing weight so use what matches your patient.

Weight Management

This weight management intervention can apply to all your patients that do not have a medical problem diagnosed as a part of the weight problem. Start this intervention once your patient is at somnambulism. Expect to reinforce this intervention in future sessions.

Because you are now at peace and relaxed, you can be successful at reaching any goal, at losing weight…you can imagine that you have lost the amount of weight you no longer want or need, and you have maintained that weight loss…You imagine and feel and think of yourself as slimmer, thinner, muscles tight, total body in shape. Your unconscious will now act on this image, and realize and actualize this image. You will allow yourself to lose weight, lose the amount of weight you no longer want or need, and to maintain that weight loss. You change negative eating patterns into good eating patterns now…you allow this to take place easily and effortlessly, and now you imagine for a moment a table, a table in front of you, and you fill this table with foods that are harmful to you, foods that are harmful to your body and emotions…you imagine these foods; they are sweets, snack foods and junk foods, you place them on the table…these foods are all harmful to you, they are like poison in your system…these kinds of foods cause you to gain weight you no longer want or need. If you choose to eat any of these foods, you eat a small amount, a very small amount of these foods satisfies you completely. You couldn't eat another bite. So now you push these foods off the table, push them away from you…your body rejects these foods. Your mind and emotions reject these foods, you clear the table, now on that empty table, and you place the many foods that you enjoy anyway. Good healthful foods, foods that contain fewer calories, there are the fruits that you enjoy, cool, clean and crisp. There are the vegetables that you enjoy, you see those good healthful foods on the table, and you imagine those good foods, and you eat slowly, very slowly, and you eat modest portions and then stop, and that feels fine. You eat correct and reasonable amounts, and you are totally satisfied, you are satisfied from one meal to the next, and have no desire to snack between meals. You feel totally proud of yourself, you reflect on all the positive things in your life, the goals and successes you have already achieved, and you know that you will continue to be successful, reaching every goal that you have, and creating the most healthy and positive life for yourself, and now you imagine seeing yourself, stomach flat, hips and thighs firm and slim…you look great and feel so good. You are relaxed and peaceful, and food is less and less important, and you are more comfortable eating slowly…snacking is unimportant to you, regardless of where you are, or what you are working on, at home or at work…you can eat small amounts of food in a restaurant, and you will eat more slowly…you may leave part of your meal on your plate, and that is fine…regardless of stress, you are more at peace and relaxed, and food is less important to you. You feel proud of yourself, the rewards are tremendous, and now whenever you think of eating, you choose those good healthful foods, and you eat the correct amount. When you have eaten the correct amount you stop eating, you can stop eating. You may even leave some food on your plate, and that is alright. You simply stop eating, and continue to relax and allow that sense of confidence and peace to now flow through you. You are more motivated now than ever before to create the most healthy and positive life for yourself, to change old eating patterns into good eating patterns, to lose the amount of weight you no longer want or need, and to maintain this weight loss. You now have new ways of dealing with your old habits, these new habits will make permanent weight loss possible. You feel wonderful, and you can begin to experience a new and healthy vital energy that flows through your body and mind, and your thoughts are positive, confident. You reflect on all the positive aspects about yourself, your intelligence and creativity, and you see yourself as the attractive person that you are, and you allow these positive feelings to grow stronger and stronger for you every day, every night, and now you continue to relax.

(Terminate trance or continue to reinforce positive self-esteem for the patient)

The View of Life

The purpose of this exercise is to provide the individual and the therapist a better understanding of the individual and how they are oriented to life. This should provide significant insight for the individual into where they are in dealing with life and problems.

Begin with taking the patient down into trance, medium stage would be appropriate.

Tell the patient the following story: (Wherever you find a number in parenthesis, this denotes the recommended pause in seconds before moving on with the script)

Now I want you to picture yourself approaching a wall, this wall can be any size, shape, color or texture that you want it to be. Take time now to notice the wall. What does it look like? What does it feel like? Is it hot or cold? Does it have a smell? (12) Now you must cross the wall, you can use anything you want to cross to the other side, the only thing you can't do is blow-up the wall. (8) Now you find yourself in a nice forest setting, as you stroll down through the forest you can notice the tall trees and pretty flowers along the way. (4) Now you find yourself coming up to a river, you pause there to look at it. This can be a flow of water anywhere, because you have seen this flow of water before. (4) Now is the time for you to prepare for your journey up stream to the source of the water. You can take any thing you want with you on your journey to the source. (6) Now you have started your journey up stream in search of the source. (10) Now you are approaching the source of the water. (4) Now that you are at the source of the water, I want you to closely examine it. (6) Now its time for you to go back down stream. You slowly turn away from the source and start your journey back. (4) Along the way you notice a bit of a beach in front of you, I want you to stop there briefly now that you are on the beach doing whatever you want to do. (12) Now its time for you to leave the beach and continue back down stream. (4) As you continue back down stream you see the place where you started from. (4) Now you step back into the forest and walk back down the path until you see the wall again. (4) Now you are standing in front of the wall again, examine it closely now. (4) As before, you need to go to the other side of the wall now by any means you choose. (6) Now you are standing on the other side of the wall where your journey first begin.

Now bring the client back up from trance. Check their orientation to ensure that they are out of trance.

Explain the following meanings to them about what they encountered on their journey:

The first wall represents your natural wall of defenses to others in the world around you.

The forest represents nothing, a transition from the wall to the water.

The river/flow of water. This represents your flow of life as you are experiencing it presently.

The source of the river/flow of water represents your very life essence. Your source of energy, motivation, etc.

What you did on the beach represents your ability to play.

The second wall represents your present defenses in life.

Child Birthing

---◆---

Most women describe the memory of giving birth to a child as a blur in their memory that seems un-recallable after they have the child. The birthing process is accomplished with and without drugs every day. As time goes on more women want to give birth to their children without the benefit of drugs. The natural method has its drawbacks; pain and discomfort are at the top of the list.

The practice of women giving birth to children under the influence of hypnosis is being used more as time passes. The Europeans seem to be the front-runners in the medical application of hypnosis. There have been numerous other cases published involving child birthing and hypnosis. This case by no means infers that medical treatment by a doctor should be bypassed.

This case involves a young couple we will refer to as Karen and David. Karen presented as a healthy 24-year-old pregnant female being seen regularly by her physician. It was Karen and David's desire to experience child-birthing without drugs. At the initial consultation she was three months into her pregnancy without complications. They explained to me that some friends of theirs had recommended trying hypnosis to expedite the healing and bypass the majority of the pain during labor and delivery. Karen and David had discussed this with their family physician, and he had referred them to me for consultation on the matter.

As David had voiced his concern about wanting to be an active participant in the birth of their child, we arrived at the decision to train David as the hypnotherapist. David appeared to be a good candidate for the role as he was a college graduate working as a Vocational Rehabilitation Counselor. He felt this training would also be valuable in his career as a Counselor. The following weekend I had scheduled a Hypnotherapy Certification Workshop that I enrolled him in to acquire the needed skills to begin working with his wife.

David eagerly attended the hypnotherapy training, and was fast to pick up on the basic techniques of Ericksonian Hypnosis. Upon his completion of the Hypnotherapy Certification Course, I started working with them as a couple. The first session was to sensitize Karen to the hypnotic trance. With the three of us in the office I first hypnotized Karen, and then turned her over to David and instructed him to use Vogt's Refractionalization method with her. The first session went very well, and Karen proved to be a very good hypnotic subject. They were instructed to continue practicing trance induction and deepening while they waited for their next appointment in one week.

For the second session I had David focus on giving Karen a post hypnotic suggestion to induce trance. During the session I had David trigger the post hypnotic suggestion three times, and deepen the trance each time. Karen had turned out to be a delightful subject to work with, and she reported how much she was enjoying the relaxation effects that accompany trance. David seemed very pleased with himself and his newfound skills.

David and Karen's physician had requested a consultation with me on this matter. I called and made an appointment, and when I visited with him in person I discovered his chief concern was any possible liability in using hypnosis. His concern was valid, and I put his mind at rest. He did have an interest in the use of hypnosis, but no real training in the field. We discussed at length the possible uses of hypnosis with a variety of medical problems. His curiosity and interest in hypnotherapy were certainly peaking, and he expressed a desire to investigate the subject more after seeing how the child-birthing went with Karen and David. I left the subject open for him and encouraged him to contact me with any concerns about hypnotherapy, or Karen and David.

Over the next four sessions with Karen and David I focused on teaching and having David practice anesthetizing Karen. These sessions were spread out over two week intervals. During these intervals they were to practice at home. Karen reported that a nice side effect of the hypnosis was that it helped her manage her morning sickness and general body discomforts. As a couple they seemed to be adhering to the treatment plan and making marvelous progress. David's skill with hypnosis had certainly developed well. When Karen and David came in for session six they reported that earlier in the week they had seen their family physician and demonstrated their hypnotic technique for the doctor. They were justifiably proud and reported that they felt their doctor was impressed. As time drew nearer for the baby's arrival the more nervous David had become. He was starting to question his own ability to follow through with the hypnosis when labor started. I talked at great length with him and reassured him that he could handle the situation when it arose. To help reinforce his self esteem and keep him occupied I had gave him homework assignments to do. First, he was to continue his hypnotic practice with Karen, then in the meantime he was to develop a written script for himself should he need it. The scripts were to cover the induction, anesthesia, pain management, and controlling the flow of blood.

Karen and David's last session with me was during the second week of Karen's ninth month. During this session I had David demonstrate these hypnotic interventions on Karen in my office so I could evaluate his proficiency. Every thing checked out well. David's proficiency was excellent, and Karen was extremely well sensitized now. The only remaining thing to accomplish was the birth of the baby. Karen reported that her physician has insisted that they have an anesthesiologist standing by in the delivery room. Karen and David were both a little offended with that idea, and sounded more determined than ever for the hypnosis to work for them. I reassured them, and also provided them with my home telephone number to call me day or night if they felt they need to talk with me.

It seems that babies have no sense of time or schedules at all. About one week later Karen went into labor; it was roughly 10:30 pm when I got the phone call from David. They were at the hospital, and Karen was being prepped for the delivery. David sounded like he was confident and in control of his situation. He asked me if I would come down to the hospital for moral support. Since this was an excellent opportunity to intervene with the medical community, I had decided to go to the hospital.

When I arrived at the hospital forty-five minutes later I discovered I was too late! Karen and David were already the parents of a healthy baby boy! I caught up with David and their doctor in the maternity waiting room. David was beaming with pride. He reported that he and Karen had used hypnosis just as they had practiced, and every thing went off wonderfully. Their family doctor was also quite pleased that the delivery was without problems and without the use of drugs.

In conclusion, the hypnotic intervention was successful and had a positive impact on the local medical community. About one month after Karen delivered the baby I saw her once for postpartum depression at the request of her family physician. A six month follow up showed that mother and baby was doing well, and no problems noted. David still does some occasional trance work with his wife for headaches and stress reduction. In another three years they plan to have a second child, and intend to use hypnosis in the birthing process. Teaching the husband hypnosis and installing him as the hypnotherapist was an unusual approach, but time and individual motivation was on my side in this situation. For the sake of a better example, please refer to the following metaphoric scripts that follow. The metaphors are presented in a double spaced format for ease of use.

Transient (Brief) Pain Management

You are sitting there comfortably aware that you have come here today because you want to gain control of your own abilities, to eliminate some future feelings of discomfort, and as you continue to relax and to drift down into a deep trance, I want you to take your time, not too fast, not too slow, because there are some things you need to listen to carefully, first you need to understand that you already have the ability to lose an arm or a hand, to become completely unaware of exactly where that arm is positioned, or what it is doing, and you have the ability to be not concerned about exactly where that arm is, or that hand or leg, or your entire body for that fact, this may seem to take too much effort to pay attention to at times, because you also have an unconscious ability you can learn how to use effectively, and that ability is to turn off the feeling in an arm, a leg, or anywhere you chose, and once you discover how it feels to not feel anything at all, wherever you want that to occur, then you can create the numb, comfortable feeling, anywhere, anytime it is useful to you, and I don't know whether your unconscious mind will allow you to discover that numb feeling in the right hand, or a finger of the left hand first, a tiny area of numbness, a comfortable tingling feeling, a heavy thick numbness, that seems to grow and spreads over time, until it covers that hand, the back of the hand, or anything else you pay close attention to, it's your choice, it just seems to disappear from your experience, but you don't know how it feels, to not feel something that isn't there, so here is what I want you to do, I want you to reach over to that numb area, to that numb hand, that's right, go ahead and touch it (pause), and feel that touching as you begin to pinch yourself there, at first you may experience a feeling, but as you continue to pinch yourself, an interesting thing happens. You begin to discover that there are times when you feel nothing at all there, that's right, the feeling just seems to disappear, as you continue to learn how to allow your unconscious mind to turn off those feelings, all you need to do is just pay very close attention to the numbness, and as that ability grows and develops, and you begin to know, really know beyond a doubt, that you already do know how to allow feeling and pain to disappear from your hand, or anywhere, your other hand can return to a resting place of its choice, and you can drift up to that point where wakeful awareness will return, so go ahead now, as you relax, and discover how to let go and to feel that numbness more and more clearly, and you can drift up more, in your own time, in your own comfortable way, that's right, take your time to learn, and then drifting back upwards, eyes opening (pause) now, before you wake up completely, I would like you to close your eyes again, and allow that drifting down again, reentering that place of calm relaxation, perhaps going even deeper than before, while you drift down again, there is a story I want to tell you about a young boy on TV not long ago in the past, he had learned to control all of his pain, he described the steps he went down in his mind, one at a time down those steps, until he found this hall at the bottom, like a long tunnel, and all along the tunnel on both sides were many different switches, switchboxes, each clearly labeled, one for the right hand, one for the left, one for the leg, and one for every place on the body, and he could see the wires to those switches clearly, the nerves that carried the feelings from one place to another, all going through those switches and switchboxes, all he needed to do was to reach up in his mind and turn off the switches he wanted to, and then he could feel nothing at all, no feelings could get through from there, no feelings at all, because he had turned off those switches, he used his mind's abilities differently from the man who simply made his body numb, he didn't know how he did it exactly, all he knew was he relaxed and disconnected, like a train car disconnecting from the rest, moved his mind away from his body, moving it outside some place else, where he could watch and listen, but drift off some place else, and it really doesn't matter exactly how you tell your unconscious what to do, or how your unconscious does it for you, the only thing of importance is that you know you can lose the feelings as easily as closing your eyes, and drifting down within, where something unknown in the unconscious happens that allows you to disconnect from the uncomfortable feeling, that allows that numbness to occur.... and then a drifting upwards now, upwards towards the surface and slowly allowing the eyes to open as wakeful awareness returns with a comfortable continuation of that protected feeling of safe, secure relaxation and an ability to forget an arm, or anything at all, with no need to pay attention to things that are just fine, that somebody else can take care of while you drift in your mind,remaining secure in this new knowledge you have gained (pause), now it is time to enjoy that comfortable drifting upwards where the eyes open, and wakeful awareness returns quite completely now.

If possible, before the client leaves your office, ask him to practice making a body part numb. Ask the client to practice this as much as reasonably possible before the next session. Future sessions may or may not require repeating this practice.

Lingering Memories

◆

PTSD, otherwise known as Post Traumatic Stress Disorder has become almost a common problem in our society. PTSD is found in victims of rape, auto accidents, violence and molestation. The most well known or highly publicized PTSD is veterans of combat.

This case deals with a thirty two year old, right-handed, Caucasian single female who was rape victim. The patient reported having been violently raped at age 19, and still plagued today with recurring nightmares and flashbacks to the incident. The patient was referred by a former patient who was a close friend of hers. For the sake of confidentiality we will call this person Patty. This was Patty's first attempt to get professional help for this problem. At first she was very reluctant to see me as I represented a male dominant figure. Once her fears were addressed and resolved, we were able to move onto gathering information. Patty expressed a great fear of losing control of herself and her situation.

The following historical information was furnished by the client. At age nineteen she was staying with her aunt and uncle while she was starting a new job and saving money to move out on her own. One evening after she went to bed her uncle entered her bedroom and forcibly had intercourse with her. She reported being in pain, frightened, and threatened by her uncle if she told anyone. The following day she moved in with a girlfriend that she worked with to escape the situation. Since that time she also reported not being able to enjoy a healthy sexual relation-ship. With any of her boyfriends in the past, she reports thoughts of the rape intruding during intimate moments, and sometimes unable to complete intercourse or orgasm.

The uncle that raped her had died three years ago. When Patty spoke of her uncle she verbalized a great deal of anger and frustration. She was still blaming herself and upset that she didn't take more appropriate action at the time. The previous year she reported having a complete medical checkup and any physical problems ruled out. She currently has a boyfriend whom she reports has been patient and understanding with her. It appears that the importance of this relationship was the driving force that prompted her to seek therapy for this problem. Patty and her boyfriend were engaged to be married in five months and they wanted to have this problem cleared up prior to getting married. Currently they were not living together, but spending three to four nights a week at her place. I asked Patty to vividly recall the night of the rape in detail. Her memory appeared very clear and she displayed phys-ical signs of PTSD. By now the time was up for this session, and I asked Patty to return in four days with her boyfriend.

For this next session Patty appeared with her boyfriend as I had requested. They both presented as open and honest in their answers and motivation. Her boyfriend whom we shall call Ralph, was very candid with his responses. First we discussed their lovemaking in detail. There seemed to be adequate foreplay before intercourse, and reasonable after-play practiced. This ruled out any sexual similarity between the past and present. I asked Ralph to explain what he observed when Patty experienced these flashbacks. Ralph explained the occurrences as hap-pening only during actual intercourse, close to seventy five percent of the time and increasing with the passing of time. He went on to explain that she would start sobbing and say, "Stop, stop". It had become appar-ent that their emotional and sexual relationships were compatible, so now it was time to move onto trance work.

At Patty's request Ralph remained in the office during the trance work. Patty had never been hypnotized before so I started with Voit's Refractionalization Method to sensitize her to trance and establish a good working depth for age regression. Slowly I took her back to age nineteen, to the Christmas prior to the rape. From there we moved forward in time to her aunt and uncle's house. She could see herself lying in bed in the dark sleeping lightly. I reminded her that she was in control of the situation, she could say and do what she wanted, and everything would be okay. I told her now her uncle had entered her bedroom and she could tell him whatever she wanted to. There was a slight pause and Patty blurted out, "Go away and don't touch me, go". For a few seconds she appeared very tense, and then suddenly all the muscle tension was gone. I allowed her a few minutes to relax and then brought her back up from trance.

Upon questioning her about what happened in trance, Patty related much of the circumstances as before, except that when she told her uncle to go away, he left the room without touching her. She seemed quite pleased with this outcome and reported feeling empowered. As we talked more about the original circumstances of the rape I noticed a sharp reduction in her physical activity as she talked. I took this as a validation that some positive change had occurred. My main concern for Patty was just how much change had occurred. With that thought in mind I scheduled an appointment for her to return to see me for a follow-up the next week

Patty kept her scheduled appointment with me the following week. She reported that she and Ralph had sex five out of the last eight days. Patty was mildly disturbed that during two of the five sexual encounters she experienced flashbacks to the rape. Patty reported that these flashbacks were quite minor compared to the past and she was generally pleased with the improvement.

I asked Patty to describe in detail what she seen during these two brief flashbacks. In both instances she described these flashbacks as seeing her uncle's face above her face, and then it would disappear. She went on to relate that these two incidents were so brief that she didn't ask Ralph to stop intercourse, although her sexual interest had waned.

For this trance intervention I induced a light trance and took her through the NLP procedure known as the "Swish Pattern". By using a light trance we were able to negate the physical symptoms of PTSD. NLP, otherwise known as Neuro Linguistic Programming, has developed an intervention for PTSD known as the "Swish Pattern". This procedure has a positive acceptable picture overtake and replace the negative image. This intervention only requires a few minutes of time to perform. After that was completed I re-induced trance and reinforced her self-esteem and self-control. With this completed I scheduled another appointment for her to return the following week to check her progress.

In conclusion, when Patty returned the following week she was very delighted to report no further incidents of flashbacks! Patty explained that she and Ralph were totally delighted with the outcome and their lives felt normal now. To follow up I asked her to contact me prior to the wedding in four months to see if the symptoms reappeared. About four months later Patty stopped by my office to leave me a wedding invitation and report no further problems with her flashbacks.

The following metaphoric script is offered as a sample of and intervention with PTSD patients. It is presented in a double spaced format for ease of use.

Dreams

Now you have told me many things about your life, and listening to the truth about someone's life is a privilege and an honor, and though you don't need my thanks, I really do thank your conscious mind for sorting and categorizing so much information, and I thank your unconscious mind for what you can let your conscious mind

discover later on, and there are so many things a person can discover,
I remember the time five or six years ago when I first discovered what
it would be like to live an entire life feeling different every day,
because that's when I met Annie, and she was the only dwarf I'd ever
met, and I learned that in childhood it really hadn't been a problem
because everyone was small and little then, but friends grew up and
Annie stayed small, and had to go living her life in a world of big people, she had a special stool in the kitchen, she pushed it around as she
moved from counter to cabinet, so she could jump on top of it and
reach out for the things she needed, so she could look into the freezer,
and reach the burners on the stove, she had a special sewing machine
and she made all of her own clothes from her own designs since
nothing else would fit, I really wanted to learn from her about living
such a life, and she told me, there's just one thing you can say about
people like me, there's always going to be something that comes up,
and I thought a long time about that and what it might mean in a life,
now a client I worked with a while back told me about a dream he
had where he'd awaken in his bedroom, but the entire room was covered with a dense fog, and when he first felt the fog he was quite
angry, finding himself damp and uncomfortable and unable to see a
foot ahead of him, and the anger just grew and grew until he felt
nothing but rage, and that heavy fog enveloping him, he wanted to
run screaming from the room, but when he opened his mouth to
speak nothing came out, and who would he tell? He was so alone, and
how could there be so much fog? Would anyone believe him? These
thoughts occupied his mind, he couldn't move, he couldn't cry, he
could only feel his anger, rusting like a nail in the dense fog, and just
when things seemed darkest he became aware of a breath of warm air
hovering around his face, and you can imagine his surprise to discover
that warm air, moist air was his own breath mingling with the fog, and
he continued to breathe, deep strong breaths, blowing that fog away
with every inhalation as the fog lifted, and light began filtering into the

room, anger lifting, breathing calmly, peacefully, and he awaken from that dream with a new understanding, and it was about the same time that his sister received a letter about the inheritance, now he and his sister were orphaned at a very early age, and they had impressed upon me that their expectations from childhood didn't include having anyone look out for them, or take care of them, they were all alone in the world, on their own in the world, or so it seemed to them, until the day they got the letter telling them they were to receive a large inheritance, and their puzzlement grew and grew, since they were orphans, alone in the world, but adults so often forgot the things they knew so well as children, just as they had forgotten the times they'd save a penny here, a nickel there, and left them for safe-keeping with a kind old woman up the street, who had taken their money and invested it with her own until she could return their own savings to them multiplied into the thousands and thousands, and with so many resources to rely on, a child, robbed of a parent, became rich as an adult, safe and comfortable now, and though sometimes you dream in darkness, that is one of your lives by now, it is not the time you know best, so much of the journey has been in shadow, now you are safe, you now know life in light, where there is no pressure, no rush to change, only the time without shadows.

The Journey of Learning

This intervention allows the patient to look into their mind's eye to the future so they may decide for himself what behavioral changes they wish to address.

Picture yourself walking slowly down the mountain, becoming more relaxed with each step you take, each breeze that caresses your body relaxes you more and more, the path is made up of switchbacks, and each time you change direction you'll double your relaxation (Pause). You're about a third of the way down the mountain, enjoying every step, feeling a comfortable breeze blowing, keeping you not too hot and not too cool, but just right. You stop and look up at the clouds against a beautiful blue sky, take a deep breath now, and peacefulness overtakes you and you continue down, deeper down the mountain. You've become more relaxed with each step that is taken, allowing every muscle in your face, neck and shoulders to let go of any tension. Your legs and feet feel great; walking down the mountain brings pleasure to your heart and body (Pause). You are half way down the mountain, you see a place to stop and take a break, there is a tree and a stream and you are able to watch the birds fly about, taking some time to relax yourself deeper, deeper relaxed than you've been before...(Pause) its now time to journey to the bottom of the mountain and relax much more deeply now, down, down slowly deeper down the mountain in complete joy, peace, strength and energy. Nothing bothers you, nothing disturbs you in any way the peace that passes all understanding is your feelings of love and acceptance of who you are, are yours. as you reach the bottom of the mountain you notice a fork in the path. You must make a decision which path to take. If you go to the left, you will experience your future with no changes. If you choose to go to the right, you can experience the changes you want to make now...first let us experience the left path, keeping all your behaviors, beliefs, and attitudes, see what your life is like for you now. What is it costing you physically, emotionally spiritually and financially? (Short pause) How do you feel? What do you say to yourself? (8-second pause) Now go 5 years into the future. Look at yourself in the mirror; are you happy with what you see? (Short pause) What are your behaviors costing you? Financially, emotionally, socially and spiritually? (5 second pause) How do you feel about yourself? (Pause) What are you saying to yourself while you look into the mirror? (Pause) Now lets go ten years into the future. Look at yourself in the mirror, are you happy with what you see? (Pause) What are your behaviors costing you? Financially, emotionally, socially and spiritually? (Pause) How do you feel about yourself? (Pause) What are you saying to yourself while you look into the mirror? (Pause) Now I want you to go to the time when you're rocking in a rocking chair and reflecting on your whole life, what do you say to yourself? (Pause) What do you wish you had done differently? (Pause) What behaviors do you wish you had changed? What attitudes have hindered you? What beliefs about you and others have limited you? Is this the life you wanted? What learning can aid you back in the present? (Pause) Come back now to the cross-roads and let's travel the path to the right. Take a couple of nice deep breaths, letting go. Now in your mind's eye experience yourself making the changes that are important to you (pause). Who you are tomorrow depends on the decisions you make today. Behaviors you want to change, beliefs about yourself that are limiting you. What new beliefs could you now believe about yourself and others? (Pause) What new attitudes can enhance your life? (Pause) Now let's journey one year into your future, look in the mirror. See some of the positive changes that have taken place. How do you feel? (Pause) What do you say to yourself? (Pause) How have these changes affected you emotionally, socially, physically and financially? (Pause) What other areas in your life are different? (Pause) Now go five years into the future, look at yourself in the mirror, how happy are you with the changes you've made? (Pause) How have the changes affected you? (Pause) look into that mirror, what do you say to yourself? (Pause) Now go ten years into the future, look at yourself in the mirror, how happy are you with the changes you've made? (Pause) How have the changes affected you? (Pause) Look in to the mirror, what do you say to yourself? (Pause) Now go twenty years into the future, look at yourself in the mirror, how happy are you with the changes you've made? (Pause) How have the changes affected you? (Pause) Look into the mirror, what do you say to yourself? (Pause) Now go fifty years into the future, look at yourself in the mirror, how happy are you now with the changes you have made? (Pause) How have these changes affected you? (Pause) Look into the mirror again, what do you say to yourself? (Pause) Now I want you to go to the time when you are rocking in a rocking chair, reflecting on your whole life. See how making one or two changes can make a difference on the outcome of your life. A change in a behavior, belief or attitude can have a rippling effect in many ways and in many areas of your life. How is your life richer financially? (Pause) How is your life richer spiritually? (Pause) What have been the benefits in terms of significant others, family, friends and others? (Pause) What other areas of your life have you improved? (Pause) Now what are you saying to yourself? (Pause) How do you feel about yourself knowing changes have taken place? (Pause) What is it like to look in the mirror at yourself? Enjoy it, intensify it! Come back to the present, today, and know that all of it is yours; the choices are yours, (Terminate trance)

To be Phobic

———————— ◆ ————————

Phobias abound; there have been countless articles and books written on the subject of phobias. Most written material touts one form or another of therapy to deal with phobias. To my knowledge there have never been any extensive research on which course(s) of treatment has the highest success rate. At the risk of sounding like a rebel rouser, I feel much of this therapy is too lengthy and far too costly. Many therapists have confided in me that their choice of treatment for their patients is largely determined by the patient's ability to pay and short treatment equals short income! That has been the downfall that plagues the use of hypnosis and NLP, as it is usually a quick and effective intervention. In the following case history I chose to treat a phobic with the combination of Nuero Linguistic Programming (NLP) and Ericksonian Hypnosis. I strongly favor the use of NLP as it is quick, effective, and many interventions can be done in or out of trance. Ericksonian hypnosis and NLP can only enhance a counselor's therapeutic toolbox.

This patient whom we shall call Troy, was self-referred due to his problems with agoraphobia. Troy was a thirty seven year old married white male employed as an industrial tool salesman. He was responsible for a sales area that covered four states. Up to the point of coming to see me, he had limited all of his traveling in the four state areas to driving his company car. Troy had been successful in his job despite the tremendous amount of driving he did over the past three years. To reward him for his hard work the company was promoting him to regional manager where he would be responsible for a ten state area. This forced Troy to face up to his fear of flying. His new job would require him to take airplane trips two or three times a month. Up to this point he had been successful in avoiding situations where he would be flying, but now he feels compelled to seek treatment to secure his new career move.

Troy reported his only attempt at flying was about seven years ago. He had gone to the airport to catch his flight. Before he could board the flight he became panicky and ran from the airport. Everywhere he went, he drove or took the train to his destination. He had accepted this modification in his lifestyle, and flying was no longer a problem in his life. Fortunately for Troy, all of his relatives and his wife's relatives lived in their local area. As Troy explained all of his feelings and reactions when he had been at the airport seven years ago. all the symptoms of a phobic reaction were there. For this initial session I mainly focused on the details of the interview and did a brief trance induction.

This way Troy would have some understanding of what the trance experience was like. We scheduled an appointment for him to return in four days. The treatment intervention I had planned was the use of a Nuero Linguistic Programming (NLP) intervention known as the "Fast Phobia Cure". I have had numerous successes with this intervention in the past. NLP has been around for quite some time now, but it has been very slow in gaining credibility as a form of therapy. My more traditional colleagues tend to shy away from the use of NLP. It is largely considered as still a radical form of therapy, and the second complaint oddly enough is, it works too fast! Another wonderful thing about these NLP interventions is that you can use them in or out of trance. I find that to be a real bonus as some patients are extremely reluctant to be hypnotized. When Troy returned in four days we immediately launched into trance work. I took Troy down to a medium state of trance and began the intervention. First I asked him to see himself walking into a movie theater and looking around, seeing the movie screen to his left and the projection booth to his right, with all the rows of seats in between. Then I asked him to see himself walking to the middle of the theater and have a seat facing the movie screen. Once that was done I asked Troy to imagine that he was floating out of his body and back into the projection booth, seeing himself still sitting there in the middle of the theater. Now I asked him to see the last phobic incident he had on the movie screen in a black and white picture of himself just prior to the phobic situation. Once that was accomplished I asked Troy to leave the projection booth and walk down the aisle past himself to the movie screen and step into the still black and white picture. Now I asked him to turn the picture into color and play the movie at normal speed through the phobic incident to a point of safety afterwards. At this time I observed Troy squirming a bit and his face grimacing, and then he relaxed. Now I asked him to play the movie backwards as fast as he could, maybe two seconds or less to the point just prior to the phobic incident. When Troy accomplished this I could see facial muscles moving and then relaxing. To test the results I asked him to play the movie through at normal speed seeing himself going through this phobic situation. Troy's reaction was nearly nil compared to the first time. Once again I asked him to play the movie backwards as fast as he could. This time there was no reaction present. Now I instructed Troy to leave the theater and travel to his special place to relax even deeper.

After bringing Troy out of trance, he reported remembering everything that was said. He stated he felt no differently than before. At this time we asked Troy's wife, who was in the waiting room to join us. Troy felt he needed to validate the treatment to know for sure if it worked. I encouraged him and his wife to validate this experience as soon as possible, but to expect some nervousness to be present, but expect the symptoms of the phobic reaction to be present. They left my office to go to the local airport to check on Troy's response, and were to return to see me the same afternoon with their conclusion.

Troy and his wife returned in about two hours to my office. They were happy to report that he could actually enter an airplane without the fight or flight response being present. Troy did state that he was quite nervous, but was able to respond in a healthy manner. I reinforced for him that the nervousness was a normal response, and encouraged him to take a short flight as soon as possible to reinforce his success. Before departing I told Troy to return if the problem should recur.

Telephonically I followed up with Troy to see what his current status was. He had received his promotion to the new job, and now flies two to three times a month in the performance of his job. He also stated that his nervousness has greatly subsided and no problems noted.

While this "Fast Phobia Cure" seems unusually fast, it has always proven to be effective for my clients. I have been and will always continue to be an advocate of NLP as a treatment approach. NLP evolved from the study of such greats in our field as Virginia Satir, and my personal favorite, Dr. Milton Erickson.

The following hypnotic scripts that were used in the treatment of phobias are offered for your information. You will find some patients will need this type of deep relaxation to be able focus better on their problems.

Deep Muscle Relaxation Training

This is phase one of three phases. The Muscle Relaxation Phase and Guided Imagery Phase follows this script and should be taught in this order. This is particularly good for your patients who have trouble relaxing.

The number of seconds to pause is denoted by the number in parentisis

Welcome to this session, during the next 30 minutes we will work our way through deep muscle relaxation training. The end result of this session is for you to have a heightened sense of awareness of what your body feels like to be fully relaxed. This technique alone will not teach you every thing you need to know. It is imperative that you practice all three phases of this program.

We will begin by having you assume a comfortable position. You can either be sitting down in a chair or lying down. If you use a chair, try to make it one with arms, if lying down, do not use a pillow. If your clothing is too tight and uncomfortable, loosen it slightly now (4). Settle back now as comfortable as you can (4). Focus your attention on my voice (3). As other thoughts drift into your mind, let them drift away and continue to focus on my voice only (4). (Spend four minutes talking the client through a deep breathing exercise). As you relax, clench your right fist, now clench your fist tighter and tighter, and study the tension in your right fist and forearm. You can feel the tension become uncomfortable in your right fist and forearm. You can feel the tension become uncomfortable in your right fist as you keep it tightly clenched (3). Now relax (4). Let the fingers of your right hand become loose (5). Observe the contrast in the feelings of your right hand (5). Let yourself go and try to become more relaxed all over (5). Once more again, clench your right fist really tight (3). Hold it tight (3). Now notice the tension again, it feels very tight and uncomfortable (2). Now let go (2). Relax; straighten out your fingers (3). Notice the difference once more (10). Now we will repeat that with your left hand and forearm (2). Clench your left fist while the rest of your body relaxes (3). Clench your fist tight and feel the tension (3). Now relax (5). Again, enjoy the contrast in feelings (4). Let your mind focus on that feeling of relaxation. Repeat that once more; clench your left fist (3). Make your fist very tight and tense (3). Now relax and feel the difference (4). Slowly straighten out your fingers (10). Clench both fists now (3). Tight, and tighter (2). Both fists tense, forearms tense, study the sensation (2). Relax now (2). Let the feelings of relaxation flow into both hands (2). Straighten out your fingers and feel the relaxation (3). Continue relaxing your hands and forearms more and more (3). Now bend both your elbows and tense

your biceps by pulling your hands towards your shoulders (3). Tense,
them tighter and study the feelings of tension (5). Now straighten out
your arms (4). Let them relax, and now feel the difference again (3). Let
the relaxation develop (8). Once more, tense your biceps (4). Hold that
tension and observe it carefully (4). Straighten your arms and allow the
feelings of relaxation to flow into yours arms (4). Relax to the best of
your ability (8). Now straighten your arms so that you feel the most tension in the triceps muscle along the back of your arms (3). Now relax
(5). Move your arms back into a comfortable pos4lion (5). Let the
relaxation flow on its own accord (8). Your arms should feel comfortably heavy as you allow the relaxation to flow (5). Once more,
straighten your arms so that you feel the tension in your triceps (8). Let
your arms relax again and focus on the comfortable heavy feeling of
relaxation in your arms (6). Now let's focus on pure relaxation in the
arms without any tension. Move your arms into a comfortable position
and let them relax (8). Let the relaxation flow into your arms (3). Focus
on that nice warm feeling in your arms (10). Even when your arms seem
fully relaxed, try to let your arms achieve a deeper level of relaxation
(12). Now we will move upwards to the head and shoulders (2). We will
start by letting all your muscles go loose and heavy. Just settle back quietly and comfortably. Wrinkle up your forehead now (3). Wrinkle it
tighter (5). Now stop wrinkling your forehead (4). Relax and allow it to
smooth out (3). Picture your entire forehead and scalp becoming
smoother as the relaxation increases (10). Now frown and crease your
brows and study the tension (6). Let go of the tension once again,
smooth out your forehead once more (10). Now close your eyes tighter
and tighter (5). Feel the tension (3). Now relax your eyes (4). keep your
eyes closed gently, comfortably and notice the relaxation (10). Now
clench your jaws (10). Relax your jaws now, let your lips part slightly
(6). Appreciate the feeling of relaxation (12). Now press your tongue
hard against the roof of your mouth (4). Look for the tension (4). All
right, let your tongue return to a comfortable and relaxed position (10).

Now press your lips together (4). Tighter and tighter (4). Relax your lips, note the contrast between tension and relaxation (8). Feel the relaxation all over your face (8). Now to attend to your neck muscles, press your head back as far as it can go and feel the tension in your neck (3). Roll it to the right and feel the tension shift (3). Now roll it to the left (3). Straighten your head and bring it forward (3). Press your chin against your chest (4). Let your head return to a comfortable position, and study the relaxation (5). Let the relaxation develop (10). Now shrug your shoulders straight up (4). Hold the tension (4). Drop your shoulders slowly and feel the relaxation (4). Feel your neck and shoulders relaxing (8). Shrug your shoulders up and forward (4). Now back, Feel the tension in your shoulders and in your upper back (4). Drop your shoulders slowly once more and relax (6). Let the relaxation spread deeply into your shoulders, right into your back muscles (6). Relax your neck and throat, and your jaw and other facial areas as the pure relaxation takes over and goes deeper (3). Deeper, even deeper (10). Allow yourself to focus on the warm, heavy comfortable feeling in your face and shoulders (12). If other thoughts drift into your mind, let them drift on by and continue to focus on my voice (8). We now shift our focus to the trunk of your body, start with relaxing your entire body to the best of your ability (8). Feel that comfortable heaviness that accompanies relaxation (8). Breathe easily and freely, in and out (5). Notice how the relaxation increases as you exhale (10). As you breathe out, feel that relaxation (4). Now breathe in and fill up your lungs, inhale deeply and hold your breath (4). Study the sensation (3). Now exhale, let the walls of your chest grow loose and push the air out automatically (3). Continue relaxing and breathe freely and gently (6). Feel the relaxation and enjoy it (8). With the rest of your body as relaxed as possible, fill your lungs again (8). That's fine, breath out, and again, breathe in deeply and hold it (8). Now breathe out and appreciate the relief (4). Just breathe normally (6). Continuing relaxing your chest and let the relaxation spread to your back (6). To your shoulders (6). To your neck

(6). To your arms (6). Merely let go and enjoy the relaxation (12). Now let's pay attention to your abdominal muscles, pull your stomach in (3). Pull the muscles right in and feel the tension this way(6). Now relax again, let your stomach out. Continue to breath normally, now pull your stomach in again and hold the tension (8). Release the tension (8). once more pull in your stomach fully and feel the tension (8). Now relax your stomach fully (3). Let the tension dissolve as the relaxation grows deeper (6). Each time you breathe out notice the rhythmic relaxation both in your lungs and in your stomach (10). Notice how your chest and stomach relaxes more and more (8). Try and let go of all the muscle tension anywhere in your body (12). Now direct your attention to your lower back (3). Arch up your back, make your lower back quite hollow, and feel the tension along your spine (4). Now settle back comfortably again, relaxing the lower back (10). Arch your back up again and feel the tension as you do so. Try to keep the rest of your body relaxed as possible. Try to localize the tension throughout your lower back area (2). Relax once more (3). Relax your upper back (6). Spread the relaxation to your stomach (6). Now to your chest (6). Now to your shoulders (6). Now to your arms (6). Now to your facial area (6). These parts are relaxing further and further, and further and even deeper (6). Let it flow as a warm, heavy, comfortable feeling (12). Let go of all tensions and just relax (8). Now flex your buttocks and thighs. Flex your thighs by pressing down your heels as hard as you can (6). Relax and note the difference (8). Straighten your knees and flex your thigh muscles again, hold the tension (6). Relax your hips and thighs (8). Allow the relaxation to proceed on its own (10). Press your feet and toes downwards, away from your face, so that calf muscles become tense, study that tension (6). Relax your feet and calves (8). This time, bend your feet away from your face so that you feel tension along your shins (6) bring your toes back up (2) relax again. (6) Keep relaxing for awhile (6),now let yourself relax further all over (6). Relax your feet (6). Relax your ankles now (6). Relax your calves now (6). Relax your shins now (6). Relax your knees now (6). Relax your thighs now (6). Relax your buttocks now (6). Relax your hips now (6). Feel the heaviness of your lower body as you relax still further (8). Let go now, more and more (4). Feel that relaxation all over. Let it proceed to your upper back (6). Keep realizing more and more deeply (12). Make sure that no tension has crept into your throat (2). Relax your neck and your jaws and all your facial muscles (4). Keep relaxing your whole body like that for a while. Let yourself totally relax (12). Now you can become twice as relaxed by taking in a really deep breath and slowly exhaling (6). Close your eyes so that you become less aware of objects and movements around you, and prevent any surface tensions from developing (8). Breath in deeply and feel yourself becoming heavier (6). Take a long deep breath and let it out very slowly (6). Feel how heavy and relaxed you have become (12). The relaxation is flowing thru you in a warm and comfortable way (30). In a state of perfect relaxation you should feel unwilling to move a single muscle in your body (3). Think about the effort that would be required to raise your right arm, as you think about raising your right arm, see if you can notice any tensions that might have crept into your right shoulder and your arm (6). Now you decide not to lift your arm, but to continue relaxing (12). Observe the relief and the disappearance of the tension (6). Just continue relaxing like that (12). When you wish to get up, count backward from five to one (6). You should then feel fine and refreshed, wide-awake and clam, slowly open your eyes and look about (4). Flex your fingers and toes slightly. Now in a slow and easy manner you can bring yourself to your feet (6).

It maybe necessary for you to repeat this exercise several times to develop a strong sense of awareness of what your body feels like to be relaxed. The value of this exercise is for you to develop a heightened sense of awareness of the feelings of relaxation, and the feelings of tension.

Muscle Relaxation Exercise

Welcome to the second in a series of your relaxation training. Before moving into the second phase of this program let's take a minute to review the first phase. Hopefully by now you have repeated the first phase of relaxation and tension.

During this phase I want you to mentally recall the feelings you experienced during the first session. Recall it slowly (10). Tighten and loosen your muscles if needed to re-awaken the feeling of relaxation (10). Settle back, and make yourself comfortable (15). Also recall the breathing exercises now that we are prepared (15). Lets move on(5). Begin with your feet, focus on your toes and feet, focus on that comfortable, warm, heavy feeling (10). If you find distracting thoughts drift into your mind, let them drift on by, don't try to force the thoughts out of your mind (3). Just let them drift on by (10). Focus now on the calves of your legs (10). Feel them grow heavier and heavier (10). Feel the tension drift away and that heavy comfortable feeling flow in (15). Now let that nice feeling of relaxation flow slowly upwards (15). You can feel it slowly working into your thighs (10). You're now feeling that nice warm heavy feeling spread throughout your thighs (10). Feel your thigh grow heavier and heavier (10). Feel the tension drift away and that heavy comfortable feeling flow freely (15). If you find distracting thoughts coming into your mind, let them drift on by and continue to focus on my voice (15). Let that comfortable feeling move upwards into your hips and buttocks (10). Let that mental image become warm and heavy, very comfortable (15). The feeling is becoming very soothing and relaxing (15). The feeling becomes more and more comfortable as the tension drifts away (20). Now feel that comfortable feeling move up into your stomach and lower back (10). Feel the tension start slowly drift away (10). That comfortable feeling of relaxation is starting to flow in and feels so soothing and warm (10). The feeling of relaxation continues to grow and feel warmer and more comfortable (10). Don't hesitate to let your body relax and sink into a wonderful feeling of relaxation (15). It is now traveling upwards again, into your chest and shoulders (8). The tension is now flowing away (10). The tension still slowly drifting (10). The feeling of relaxation is now taking over in your chest and shoulders (15). Spreading so slowly, and very relaxing (20). The feeling of relaxation becomes deeper and deeper (25). Now the feeling of relaxation is seeping down through your arms and into your hands (15).Now you feel your arms and hands grow warm and heavy (12). That heavy comfortable feeling is becoming more and more soothing (12). The tension has drifted out of arms and hands now, and the warm heavy feeling is flowing freely(10). Your arms and hands continue to grow warm and heavy (10). Let the feeling of relaxation go deeper and deeper (20). Now let your mind slowly move to focus on your neck and scalp (15). Let the warm comfortable feeling spread up through your neck and into your scalp (10). The tension is slowly drifting away (12). Now the warm comfortable feeling is flowing and feeling better and better (12). Slowly you feel the warmth move you deeper and deeper into relaxation (15). The feeling of relaxation is now drifting down into your facial muscles (10). The tension is drifting out now and that warm relaxed feeling is increasing (15). Now the warm heavy comfortable feeling is flowing with warmth and comfort (30). Now you are feeling that warm, heavy, comfortable feeling engulf your entire body (45). The feeling flows so freely into the warm wonderful feeling of relaxation (60). Now, very slowly count backwards from five to one (10). Now slowly move your toes (5). Now also move your fingers slightly (5). Open your eyes and slowly look about you (4).

Guided Imagery

During this session we will focus on guided imagery as a means of relaxation. This is the third and final teaching phase in progressive relaxation techniques. We start this session with a reflective look back to the sessions of deep muscle techniques and muscle relaxation. Try to recall in your mind the feelings you experienced during these exercises. The bold (0) denote pauses in seconds.

Assume a comfortable position before you begin to form the mental image of your body relaxing (6). Loosen any tight clothing and let the warm comfortable feeling of relaxation take over (12). If any distracting thoughts enter your mind, let them drift on by and continue to focus on the sound of my voice, and that warm, heavy and comfortable feeling that is starting to move through your body (15). If you have trouble recalling that feeling of relaxation at this time, stop briefly and perform phase one again of the deep muscle relaxation technique until you have developed a re-awareness of relaxation in your body (15). Now mentally recreate that feeling of relaxation in your body (10). Let it begin with your toes (10). Slowly, that warm comfortable feeling starts moving upwards (10). Now moving into the calves of your legs (10). The warm heavy feeling is flowing stronger, but quite easily (15). The feeling now moves into your thighs (10). Slowly and very warmly spreading (10). That warm comfortable feeling is now moving into your hips and buttocks (10). Slowly and warmly the feeling of relaxation is spreading throughout your lower body (10). Feel the warmth and comfort spread to your stomach and lower back (10). Feel those muscles gently let go and the relaxation flow in (15). The warm feeling of comfort is now spreading upwards through your chest and shoulders (10). Progressing gently and slowly onwards up through your neck and scalp (15). Take a minute now to dwell on the feeling you are experiencing in your body. (60) Now that you have achieved a state of relaxation , continue to focus on my voice as we create a mental picture in your mind (10). Imagine yourself now, sitting down and leaning against a huge tree in a open field (15). You are sitting in lush, soft green grass (15). You can feel a gentle warm breeze (10). The breeze is soft and warm on your face (15). Just like a soft warm caress (15). You feel very relaxed now, deeply relaxed (10). A warm comfortable feeling holds your body and mind in relaxation (15). In your mind's eye you slowly turn and look upwards (5). Looking to the top of the tree filled with leaves (10). You see that warm gentle breeze stirring the leaves on the tree, ever so softly and gently (10). You casually notice that from the top of the tree a leaf has broken away and is starting to fall (10). The warm breeze is cradling the leaf (10). Rocking the leaf gently back and forth (10). The leaf moves ever so slowly in the breeze (10). Feel that warm gentle breeze again, gently touching your face (10). Notice the free flowing relaxation going through your body (15). You also notice that the leaf is still falling ever so slowly (10). It is still being cradled and rocked, back and forth by the gentle warm breeze you feel (15). The leaf is still slowly working its way down in its descent to the ground (15). The leaf is moving so slowly and unhurried (15). Still gently floating and moving so gracefully with the breeze (15). Unhurried or bothered by time, the leaf continues its slow and deliberate descent to the ground (15). Let your mind slowly turn inward to become re-aware of the wonderful state of relaxation your body is enjoying (20). That comfortable, warm heavy feeling continues to flow through out your person (30). Now your mind slowly turns back to the leaf (5). It is still making its graceful descent downwards (15). Still gently swaying in the breeze (10). Back and forth, so slowly and gently, as it moves to its downward destination (15). With slow graceful motion, the warm pleasant breeze you feel is still carrying the leaf further downward (15). You observe the leaf moving with gentle and tender grace (15). The leaf is being cradled by the warm breeze, you can also feel the warmness of your body relaxing, and the gentle warm breeze caressing you (20). The leaf is moving slowly (10). Still making its unhurried descent to the ground below (20). The leaf is coming closer to the ground now (15). Still gently and slowly moving with an air of grace in its every movement (20). At times the leaf will appear almost to be suspended in the air by the gentle nurturing of the warm breeze (20). Now it appears to be in its final, but graceful descent (20). Slowly, with a gentle swaying motion, the leaf comes to rest beside you (10). The leaf, like you, has finally come to a complete state of rest. Mentally, let your mind explore your body in this state of relaxation (60). Now slowly count backwards from five to one (10). Slowly now, open your eyes and look about you (5). Slowly move your toes and fingers, and you will find muscle tension returning (10).

To obtain the maximum amount of effectiveness from this session, it is recommended that you repeat this exercise several times over on your own. In time, the mental image of the falling leaf will become your key to unlocking your relaxation through your mind's association with this mental image. You may in the future decide to create your own personal image to better suit your personality. I would recommend you consult with an individual in the field of psychology for assistance and guidance.

If Only It Would Stop Hurting

———————— ◆ ————————

Pain management is a problem that conventional medicine usually treats with medication in hopes that the pain will go away. Initially, medication is a good idea to maintain a person until the source of the pain can be treated in an appropriate method. Unfortunately some patients will become dependent on their medication to feel better. Therefore the pain itself has a pay value for the patient; after all, who wants to really discard a problem that will furnish them a wonderful, mind-altering drug?

Through the use of hypnosis a patient's pain can be relieved to almost any degree. Since the use of hypnosis for pain management works very well, it also has its drawbacks. The main problem I have seen with some hypnotherapists is that they will attempt to remove all the pain the patient is having. Initially they have very happy patients, but these patients are very prone to go out and do something that is going to make their injuries worse. The pain is there as nature's warning device that something is wrong. To remove the pain entirely is to also remove the warning that the body needs something repaired. Some form of a warning device should be left with the patient until the body is healed. The following case will illustrate one approach to pain management. Due to the age of this patient, she was expected to be a difficult subject to work with.

The patient was a ninety-three year old Caucasian female living by herself in a retirement community. For the purpose of this story we will refer to her as Gloria. Gloria's daughter contacted me one afternoon to request that I provide treatment to her ninety three year old mother who was suffering with pain in her shoulders from a recent fall she had. Her daughter explained that she had contacted other Hypnotherapists who had refused to treat her mother due to her age. With that kind of challenge posed to me, I couldn't pass this one up! Due to Gloria's age and current pain I arranged to make a house call with her daughter and son-in-law present. I had elicited much of the information that I needed from Gloria's daughter. I also informed her daughter that I could make no guarantees due to her mother's age, beliefs and values. If she were to note no results in her Mother, then I would not expect her to pay me.

The following morning I arrived at the retirement home and met Gloria and her daughter and son-in-law. Gloria insisted on serving me coffee before we started talking in detail. She was not reluctant to express her doubts and misconceptions about hypnosis. Patiently I explained in great detail how hypnosis worked, and answered her specific concerns. Her late husband had been a medical doctor and since he never talked about hypnosis, she was very wary of it. Finally, Gloria consented to being hypnotized on only one condition: That the Holy Bible be on the table in front of her.

To start the session, Gloria took a seat in her favorite rocking chair with a TV tray with her bible on it in between her and me. I took the bible and laid it on the middle of the tray, and placed my left hand on it, palm up. Then I asked Gloria to put her hand in mine, and listen to the sound of my voice as she gazed at the hanging plant in the corner. As I started the hypnotic patter I also started a rhythmic tapping with the index finger of my left hand that was holding her hand. Initially she resisted a bit at letting go and slipping into trance, but trance was achieved quickly and I deepened her to somnambulism without difficulty. All this time my hypnotic patter continued as did my rhythmic tapping with my index finger. To facilitate her concerns, I said many times during the trance work, "that you remain in perfect control of your situation at all times". This seemed to provide her with some additional emotional comfort that she needed.

At this time I separated her conscious from her subconscious to set the scene for the intervention. I asked Gloria's unconscious part that controlled her pain to listen closely to the new information I needed to share with it. I praised the subconscious part for doing its job so well of protecting Gloria from further pain and injury. Then I asked this part to consider trying something different to help Gloria that this would help the part do an even better job along with the wonderful job it was already doing. I asked the subconscious part that controlled Gloria's pain to provide her some relief, allow her to lift either hand above her head without pain and to be able to carefully allow Gloria to do her normal tasks without interfering, but if Gloria were to start to do something that would injure or re-injure herself, then the subconscious part was to turn up the level of pain to remind her not to do that. Everything I said I repeated twice in a positive and passive manner.

Before bringing Gloria out of trance, I reinforced for her that she still remained very much in control of her situation. Then I told her to take a few minutes for herself to think about what was said, and put it in good order. When that was accomplished she was to return to the waking state feeling rested and happy. Gloria remained in trance for the next three to four minutes before opening her eyes and looking about. Her first comment was that she would like to do trance work about once a week. It seemed her concerns and fears were no longer an issue. To test the relief from pain her daughter asked her to raise both arms above her head, which she did without effort. Prior to the start of the session Gloria could not raise either hand past shoulder height without extreme pain. Everyone seemed quite pleased with the outcome. Then I discovered something I had overlooked, her son-in-law had also slipped into trance! We all had a chuckle and then I brought him back to consciousness. I teased him and said I should charge dou-ble for two patients!

We now briefly look back on what transpired in the trance. First, holding Gloria's hand in mine on top of the bible was reassuring her of my Christian intent to help her. Secondly, by lightly tapping her hand with my index finger I was able to give a point of focus she could feel as well as see. She was then allowed to make a choice of where to fix her concentration. Thirdly, much of her fears were placated by saying sev-eral times during trance that she was in control of her situation. Before departing I talked at great length with Gloria about taking precautions to not injure or re-injure herself.

About two months later Gloria's daughter came to see me for assis-tance with her issues. She reported her mother has been doing well, her shoulders were completely healed and there were no complaints about pain. She also stated that Gloria's minister had visited with her, and upon hearing of the hypnosis asked Gloria to not subject herself to it any more, as he felt it could only facilitate the devil's work! She went on to report that Gloria gotten a good laugh out of it.

The following metaphoric example is offered as a sample interven-tion for pain management. The metaphor is presented as double spaced for ease of use.

Chronic Pain Management

Applications; long-term pain, back injuries, nerve damage, phantom limb pain, and cancer.

With your eyes closed, as you begin to relax, you probably notice that the first thing you notice is how difficult it is to not become aware of that pain and discomfort, and that's fine, you don't need to fight your mind which is always aware of those sensations there for you, because as you relax, you can begin to discover that each time you relax a muscle in your arm...or a leg...or your face...or even a foot...or a finger, that you can drift down more and more deeply than before, into that sensation there in a more relaxed and comfortable way, because there really is no need to make the effort it takes to try to stay away from that feeling or to try to fight that feeling, which almost seems to guide and direct aware-ness down toward it, more and more into it, and as you drift toward it, toward that center of that feeling, everything else can be allowed to relax, to relax more and more, as you begin to discover that it really is okay to let go in that way, to allow yourself to relax every other part of your body and to drift down toward the very tiniest center of that feel-ing, the very small middle of it, the source of it, and then to drift down through that center into a place beneath it of quietness and calm aware-ness, down through that feeling, and out the other side, into a space of relaxed letting go, of comfortable relaxation, where the mind can drift, the way waves drift from one place to another as that body relaxes and the mind becomes smoother and smoother, able to absorb events, even those events, easily and comfortably, to become absorbed in thoughts and images, as the mind reflects the clear wonder of a child, a young child, watching a flock of geese as they soar across the sky and fly into the mist, the rhythm of their sound becoming softer and softer, as soft as the down in a pillow in a place where you rest and relax, a most com-fortable place for a child to relax and drift into dreams through the mind, protected and safe, where the letting go allows the flow and the soft floating upwards, where the mind drifts free of things far below, and seems to soar in a sky as clear as glass, so smooth and clear that it disappears when you look into it, and what appears instead is the deep blue shine of the warm soft sun, a star far beyond that reaches out and provides that warm soft light as you drift down and experience the comfort and learn to feel the sound sleep that your unconscious mind can provide you whenever you relax and allow it to drift into a trance, because it can take you down through that feeling, into a space, that relaxed comfortable place, as you relax and allow it to do so just for you, that relief and relaxation, that drifting down through which comes to you whenever you allow it to, just as that drifting upwards occurs as well, a drifting back toward the surface of wakeful awareness, as your unconscious mind reminds you to drift up in a relaxed, comfortable way, back towards the surface now, bring with you that comfortable relaxation, that automatic change in sensation, even as the mind drifts upwards, the relaxation continues, as the mind awakens and the eyes open, but the body remains behind, relaxed, that's right, eyes open now (pause) but before you come back completely, you can close those eyes again, and feel that relaxation again, and recognize that ability, that ability to relax, to let your unconscious mind find the way to provide you with more and more comfort, more and more relaxed, letting go, that's right, aware that you can do so, anytime, anyplace you need or want to, you can return to that place, so here is what you do, later on today, tomorrow, next week, and for the rest of your life, whenever you need to or want to, you can close your eyes just for a moment, perhaps, and feel that comfortable feeling, that change in sensation return to you, and you drift into that light trance, or a deep trance, where your unconscious mind can take care of you, make things comfortable for you, and then you return to the surface of wakeful awareness, not needing to make the effort it takes to try to tell if that feeling is there or not, just as you return now back to the surface, comfortably relaxed and refreshed, remaining relaxed perhaps.

I Can't Find the Feelings

◆

This case history involves a lady who was sexually abused as a teenager, and now cannot experience an orgasm. What I feel makes this case so interesting is that one problem must be resolved before resolving the presenting complaint. By dealing with the sex abuse first we have set the stage to deal with the problem of no orgasm.

It is not really that uncommon to find that trauma is the catalyst for other problems. Some times the patient may not share the information with you about the trauma at the beginning of therapy, or may have deeply repressed the event in their subconscious. A good possible indication of this would be if you are dealing with a patient who now responds well to some of your proven techniques. For these patients it may be well worth your time to devote another session to investigate the possibility of repressed information. Among the very first things that must be done is to have the patient examined by a physician for organic complications. For females a gynecologist would be a good authority, and for males a urologist would be appropriate. If no physical problems exist, then therapy is the next order of business.

The case that we are going to examine involves a twenty-four-year old married female who presents with the complaint of never being able to orgasm during sex. We will simply refer to her as Gloria. She had been married for fifteen months, and she and her husband were both deeply concerned with this problem. Gloria's husband, Ted, had begun to feel he was not performing adequately. Both Gloria and Ted report doing everything they possibly knew, but still no orgasm for Gloria. They went on to report that they tried a wide array of positions and various forms of stimulation with no success. Gloria explained her sex life with her husband in a very caring manner. She felt he took time for adequate foreplay, and that he was able to sustain prolonged intercourse in hopes of her being able to orgasm. Gloria explained her feelings during foreplay and intercourse as "a little exciting", and feeling good.

When I asked Gloria if she had ever been sexually abused in her life, she immediately denied having ever been sexually abused. Gloria stated she had been involved in three different sexual affairs prior to marrying Ted. She went on to report that she was never able to achieve an orgasm since becoming sexually active. When asked if she could orgasm by masturbation, she denied having ever tried. At this point I felt that an appointment with a gynecologist was the next order of business. Before Gloria and Ted departed my office I had scheduled Gloria an appointment with a gynecologist to rule out any possible physical problems that may exist. Gloria was scheduled to return to my office two days after her medical appointment.

Gloria returned as scheduled with the results from the gynecologist. The doctor found no apparent physical reason for her to not have an orgasm. Gloria was somewhat disturbed with this news. She was hoping that there was some medical problem that was beyond her control.

We processed that thought for a short time until she came to the understanding that whatever was preventing her from having an orgasm was presently beyond her control, and that we would work toward her having the control she desired. At this time I rechecked her social history of relationships. She described her growing years as quite average with both parents in the home. Gloria stated that her relationship was very strong with her parents. She described her marriage to Ted in very glowing terms. Gloria described her husband as very thoughtful, caring, and easy to get along with. Once again I asked her if she could recall any past incidents of being sexually abused. As before, Gloria quickly denied any history of sexual abuse. Before ending the session I hypnotized Gloria briefly so she could become exposed to the feeling of being in trance. A return appointment was made for Gloria to return in one week. I also informed Gloria that I would have a female therapist with us for the future trance sessions, and she did not object.

For Gloria's third session and successive sessions I introduced my co-therapist and chaperone, Patty. Patty was a former student and colleague of mine. I have always made it a point to have a female co-therapist or chaperone present when doing trance work with a female patient involving sexual issues. We immediately focused the trance work in search of any possible trauma or sexual abuse that may be repressed. Once she was deepened to somnambulism, I regressed Gloria back in time to her seventh birthday party as a safe and pleasant starting point. From the birthday party we started to float slowly forward in time, scanning the past. We were able to get up to about age twelve when it was time to conclude the session. After Gloria was back up from trance she reported feeling a little melancholy from reviewing the "good old days". All the memories she could recall were pleasant ones from her pre-teen years. Gloria was scheduled to return here in one week for her next session. My co therapist, Patty and I talked about the case and decided that in the next session if no trauma was found, we would move into a direct approach with the problem. At this time I still felt that there is a strong possibility that some past trauma was responsible for Gloria's problem.

For session three we started out the same as session two. When Gloria was down to a state of somnambulism, I regressed her back to her twelfth birthday. From this point of safety we started moving forward in time very slowly. When we got to the summer she was fourteen, Gloria shifted around in her chair and her face grimaced. With that cue I started questioning her in trance. When Gloria was fourteen she had spent the summer with her grandparents in south Texas. During her summer, Gloria was able to recall her grandfather sexually molesting her on five different occasions. Gloria said she could remember reporting these incidents to her grandmother just prior to returning home. She recalled how upset her grandmother was, and that her grandmother told her that only "nasty girls" could enjoy or receive pleasure from sex! Gloria could also recall how terrible she felt on the bus ride home, feeling soiled, like a nasty girl. Gloria was able to cry and have a good expression of her feelings. Once Gloria was out of trance, we processed this rediscovered information at great length. At first, Gloria said she wished that she could not remember all the facts. We discussed the possible correlation between her sexual abuse and being non-orgasmic. The direct correlation seemed to be what her grandmother had told her, that only nasty girls could enjoy sex. Gloria was scheduled to return for another appointment, and before returning here she was to write a letter to her grandfather and grandmother. Gloria readily accepted the homework assignment.

Session four started with reviewing her letter to her grandparents, who had passed on several years ago. Gloria's letter was highly charged with a full range of emotions. To take this opportunity a step further, I asked her to read the letter out loud. This really provided Gloria another opportunity to vent her feelings. Between all the crying and weeping she was able to get the letter read in about fifteen minutes. Then trance was induced, and Gloria was deepened to somnambulism. At that point she was told that she would ride an escalator down three floors, and at the third floor she would see her grandfather standing there. Then Gloria was to tell him what she needed, and then he would fade away without a word. When Gloria was instructed to see her grandfather, she had various facial expressions, then the tears came, and then her facial muscles relaxed. After trance Gloria was debriefed and told that she had talked to both her grandfather and grandmother. Her conversation with her grandmother seemed to dominate; she told her grandmother at great length that she was not a "nasty girl" or a bad person. Gloria went on to explain that she was now feeling so relieved, as if a weight had been lifted from her. She was also anxious to tell her husband all about this experience. As we talked further, Gloria re-affirmed her right to enjoy sex with her husband, and she was determined to do just that. Over the past week she had felt that she was ignoring her husband with a lack of intimacy. Gloria was scheduled to return the following week to follow up on her progress.

At session five Gloria was eager to report that she felt her sex life had improved greatly. Gloria reported she thought she had two orgasms over the past week. Gloria and Patty discussed the orgasms and intensity. Gloria was mainly needing another woman to verify for her that she had indeed experienced orgasms. This was the final session for Gloria. She was left with the instructions that if she should become plagued with memories of her grandparents, that she was to return for an appointment.

In this case the patient was able to achieve her goal with the new knowledge of her past. Once she could understand the correlation between her grandparents and her lack of ability to enjoy sex, she was able then to move forward and begin enjoying a full and more satisfying sex life. If a search of her past had failed to reveal any sexual trauma, then a more direct approach would have been employed. The emphasis would have been on helping her develop better focus, self-esteem, and a better understanding of sexual functioning.

The following metaphoric example is offered as an intervention with patients who have sexual abuse issues:

Saying Good-Bye

This is a script/metaphor for use with adult survivors of abusive childhoods, trauma.

As you continue to relax and experience the awareness of many different things, you may begin to wonder how many different ways there are to heal a wound, a wound from long ago that never healed, but remained behind to change the way you think and feel, like a woman I know who always wondered why she was the way she was, until one day she discovered a child within, a sad child, an unhappy child, an angry hurt child from long ago, a child she always heard in the background, a child she protected and did everything for today, a child who made her feel so sad, and she would do anything to keep that child quiet, to keep that child happy, to give that child what it wanted and needed, and I asked what needed to be done, and she said she needed to say good-bye to that child, she needed to hug that child, to hold that child, and to tell that child how very, very sorry she was that those things had happened to it, she felt so badly for the pain, so badly for the fear, so badly for the anger, but she knew she had to say good-bye, finally, she had to leave it behind and go on with her life, she knew there was nothing she could do to save that child, to change the past, to undo what was, and there was nothing she could do, so she hugged the child, and said good-bye and walked away, and cried and cried. The hardest thing she had ever done was to say good-bye, leave it behind, abandon it to the past, she felt awful, but she knew that was what she had to do, all she could do was watch the child slowly disappear, there was nothing she could do to change the past, it was beyond her control now, as it was in the past, nothing she could do to undo what that child went through, but afterwards she was free, felt free, to do what she wanted, the child was gone and she was free, free of the past, free to be, and so as you relax, and continue to drift down, your unconscious knows what you can do, or not do, your conscious knows too, and you can feel the freedom of that relaxed letting go in your own way, even as you drift more deeply at times than others.

Depression, My Old Friend

◆

Depression in our society is as common as catching a cold. The definition of depression is to press down or move down and comes in different degrees of severity. The two forms that are the most debilitating are severe depression that leads to suicidal ideations, and chronic depression. In this case history we will be dealing with a patient who has suffered from chronic depression for most of his life.

For the treatment of depression there is no cure-all approach; there is a need for highly individualized treatment planning for the effective treatment of depression. To further complicate matters, I have found that most patients do not have any real knowledge why they are chronically depressed and usually express symptoms of lack of energy, low libido; sleep disturbance, difficulty concentrating, and a sense of apathy. Therefore, the root cause of the depression is the unknown variable. It could be from past traumas, or an imbalance in neuro-chemicals. If a patient you are going to treat for depression has been seeing a medical doctor prior to seeing you, it is absolutely necessary to make sure that the patient is not currently taking psychotropic drugs, or illegal drugs that would tend to mask the emotions.

The patient, Lance, is a married thirty one year old male who was self-referred due to chronic depression. Lance reports being seen by a psychiatrist for the past fourteen months with no results. He stated he had been on Prozac for a year, and now he has been off the medication for over sixty days. Lance went on to explain how his depression has been debilitating to him. He stated he felt that his libido was very low and was only able to sexually perform once a week at the very most. His sleep disturbance was described as awakening about every two hours, and remaining drowsy during the day. Lance stated that his ability to concentrate was so poor that he could not even read a newspaper article. He went on to report that he has had this sense of apathy for nearly as long as he can remember. Lance was unable to link the onset of the depression to any events in his life. Currently he is employed as a carpenter, and denies that his depression has any negative bearing on his job. Lance expressed his chief concern about his depression as his problem with a low libido. He went on to clarify that he was worried that eventually he would lose his wife if he continued to not meet his wife's needs. Lance explained that he often thought about intercourse, but found himself unable to perform. He expressed much frustration with his situation.

Lance denies having ever been hypnotized before. The idea of him seeking hypnotic treatment was his wife's. As usual, most of the initial session was devoted to history taking, and the session was wrapped up with putting Lance in trance to help sensitize him to hypnosis. Lance was scheduled to return the following week.

When Lance returned for his second session, we moved directly into trance work. Lance was deepened rapidly to a state of somnambulism. From this point we engaged Lance's unconscious parts. First we asked Lance's unconscious part that was responsible for his feelings to communicate with me. Once access was established, I asked the unconscious part to share with Lance's conscious mind what purpose the depression served (Later out of trance I would process this with Lance). The unconscious part signaled me with ideomotor signaling that it had completed the task. Then I asked the creative part of Lance's unconscious to communicate with me. I asked his creative part to come up with three new alternatives to getting Lance's needs met without the depression. It took about five minutes to accomplish this procedure. Once completed, I asked Lance's unconscious if there were any parts that objected to Lance trying any of these three new alternatives. No objection was noted at this point. Lance was then brought up from trance to the waking state.

Once that Lance was awake and completely coherent, I asked him to talk about his trance experience. Lance reported that the main thing that stood out in his mind was the purpose that his depression served. He stated that the answer seemed almost instantly apparent when I asked him in trance what purpose the depression served, and the image of his mother came to his mind. It seems that Lance's mother passed away when he was eight years old from a cardiac condition. As we talked further, it was apparent that Lance had never completed the grieving process. Now his depression was acting in place of the failed grieving process. Lance's father was an alcoholic, and after his wife's death he drank daily and moved around the country with his children in tow. About a year later his father remarried, and Lance remained in a blended family until going in the Army at seventeen. This was all quite overwhelming for Lance; some of this unresolved grief was emerging as he talked. Once Lance had regained his composure, he was given a homework assignment to complete before returning for his next session. Lance was directed to write a letter to his mother and tell her about how he felt before returning next week.

When Lance returned for session three he had three letters with him! One letter to his mother, one letter to his father, and a third letter to his stepmother! Lance explained that when he had finished the first letter he realized that there was a lot he also wanted to tell his father and his stepmother. I commended him for his work, and we went on to review the letters in detail. Lance said he had invested several hours in writing each letter, trying to express all the "mixed up" feelings he was experiencing. As today was Monday, Lance and I agreed that he would deal with each letter in a separate session: One session today, one session

Wednesday, and another Friday. We definitely had our work cut out for us now. I felt that separate sessions for each letter would be better, and would keep Lance's emotions from getting confused with the other people in this scenario.

For each of these next three sessions, Lance was put into trance and deepened to somnambulism for the work. He was told that he would ride three escalators down, and when he stepped off the third escalator he would see the person he wanted to talk to. At that time he was to express his feelings to him, holding nothing back. After he said what he felt, Lance was to step back on to the escalator coming up, and the significant other would fade away. Each of these sessions brought about a cascade of feelings from Lance. After each hypnotic session was completed, we processed what he had experienced and his present state of emotions. Lance was now reporting that on a day-to-day basis he was feeling better. By this time we had completed five sessions, and I planned on two more if everything continued to go well.

The following week Lance returned for session six. He reported feeling better, physically and emotionally. Lance also reported a slight increase in his libido, and expressed the thought that he was really starting to improve. For this session I intended for Lance to meet his "Inner Child". Lance went into trance quickly, and was again deepened to somnambulism. Lance was regressed back to the year that his mother passed away. Then I had him see himself standing outside the home where he lived with both parents. Then I told Lance to enter the house the way he used to as a child. As he entered the house he was to look around and see all the familiar things there. As he approached the living room he could see himself there as the eight year old child. Lance was instructed to tell his little boy something valuable, something he could use in the future. Once Lance accomplished this, he was told to tell his little boy goodbye, hugging him if he could before he left. After trance Lance was de-briefed about the experience. He reported that he told his inner child that it was okay to get angry, and it is okay to cry when he hurts inside. Lance was visibly moved by this experience. He was scheduled to return for follow up in three weeks. At that time we could either opt for some self-esteem work, or terminate treatment. If anything developed before his next appointment he was to call.

Three weeks later Lance showed for his scheduled appointment. This time he brought his wife with him. Lance reported virtually no problems with depression at this time. He denied any of the initial presenting symptoms that he reported in the first session. Lance's wife also went on to explain that he was like a new person with more energy.

A one-year telephonic follow-up with Lance revealed no return of his symptoms of depression, apparently still functioning very well. In this case, as with many, once the patient can develop clear insight into his problem, he is able to move forward in a more effective manner. I have not found it uncommon to discover that a good many patients present for treatment with little or no insight into their problem. Once some insight is developed, patients normally feel empowered and ready for effective forward movement in dealing with their problems.

The following metaphoric example is offered as a sample intervention with a depressed patient. The metaphor is presented in a double spaced format for ease of use.

Treasures of the Past

This script/metaphor is good for clients who are depressed or have lost a significant person in their life.

I wonder if you have ever seen the small fragile glass figurines that artisans sell at fairs and in shopping malls, made of tiny strands of clear bright glass all carefully laced together to form the shape of a ship or an animal, or even a house or a tree, that seemed to fascinate children with their delicate sparkles and shapes, like priceless jewels, valuable possessions, to be carried in velvet cases and protected, kept safe from

loss or damage, tiny treasures, a gift to someone, like the treasure
carried in ships across the sea, there was a program on TV several years
ago, about a man who spent twenty years searching for such a ship, a
lost treasure ship, one of hundreds that had been lost along the coast
because of accidents and disasters and wars, he researched it very
carefully, and though he knew exactly what had been lost, he also
thought he knew what happened and where the treasure had sunk, but
it was hard to find that ship, it had been lost for so long, it had gotten
buried with mud and coral, and there were many other wrecks in the
area, any one of which could have been the one, but wasn't, so he spent
many years searching, and he raised thousands of dollars from
investors, because he was convinced that there was something of great
value down there, a lost treasure of immeasurable worth, and he
convinced others it was there too, one day the divers returned to the
surface shouting and screaming and holding up gold bars, they had
found that ship, and it contained more than you could imagine, tons of
gold bars, silver bars, gold coins, treasures untold, things from the past
that had gone untouched, that had not been seen for hundreds of years
suddenly were there for people to hold and to feel, and they held them
with reverence, touching them gently and silently, as if these things that
had been lost for so long, contained some memory of the past,
something special that people need, something special to protect, like
those tiny glass figures that you see at fairs and malls, they seem to be
so fragile, so easily broken by someone rough, but they actually are
quite sturdy and can survive for years and years, even when lost or
hidden away, like the treasures at the bottom of the ocean, hidden deep
down below, something precious and valuable inside, a part of you
before, that belonged to you before, and the joy of its discovery, the
recovery of that buried treasure, the pleasure of knowing it belongs to
you, something you can bring back with you, that warm good part of
the heart of the matter that children sometimes lose for a time, or have

taken from them at another time, but it always lies there waiting to be brought back to the surface where it can be touched and protected and kept close to you forever, because it all belongs to you.

About the Author

◆

Randy Hartman earned his masters degree from the University of Oklahoma in human Relations. Randy has more than twenty five years in people helping profession and has a total of five books to his credit in hypnosis.

www.ingramcontent.com/pod-product-compliance
Lightning Source LLC
Chambersburg PA
CBHW020303290526
45784CB00003B/1342